A HUNDRED-YEAR WIND

A HUNDRED-YEAR WIND

Reflective Poems

Richard J. Ackerman Jr.

Copyright © 2016 by Richard J. Ackerman Jr.

Mill City Press, Inc.
322 First Avenue N, 5th floor
Minneapolis, MN 55401
612.455.2293
www.millcitypublishing.com

All rights reserved. No part of this publication may be reproduced, stored in a retrieval system, or transmitted, in any form or by any means, electronic, mechanical, photocopying, recording, or otherwise, without the prior written permission of the author.

ISBN-13: 978-1-63413-814-7
LCCN: 2016902871

Cover Design by Alan Pranke
Typeset by Jim Arneson

Printed in the United States of America

For Mona

CONTENTS

Premise	1
Transitory Advantage	2
Saturday Morning	3
Severance	4
About Face	7
Perseverance	13
How Many for How Much	14
Knowing We Don't	16
Economics Lesson	17
The Dachshund and the Greyhound	19
Mother Knew	21
Ever the Boy Who Dreamed Such a Dream	22
Second-Grade Soul	25
Four and a Half Billion Years and Counting	29
An Opportunity Prayer	30
Playing Logical God with a Nuclear Collider	31
Sprinklers that Run in the Rain	33
January Night	34
Yesterday, Today, Tomorrow	35
In the Course of a Business Day	36
Reentry	38
Bittersweet Finality	39
School Shoes	40
Barefoot Girl in a Calico Dress	43
A Hundred-Year Wind	53
Then and Now	58
Unexpected Transfer	60
In a Glass of Confidence	62
Parental Guidance	73
The Commanding General's Daughter	75

CONTENTS

Arrogance	76
Looking with the Sun	77
Hands-On Time	78
Last Reunion	85
Upward Mobility	88
Career Move	89
Life	91
Tell the Stories Now	92
Eminent Domain	93
Crux of the Matter	102
Taking Responsibility	103
Lifespan of a Newspaper Edition	104
Clearly Understood	106
Open-Minded	107
Pigeon House	108
Divorce	109
Modern Complication	110
A Middle-Class Material Legacy	113
Carryover	115
At the Bottom of a Desk Drawer	116
Oh, Boy	117
Pride	118
The Beach Hereabouts	122
In for a Penny, in for a Pound	123
Shortest Month of the Year	125
Stakeholders and Others	129
Small Business	131
Chance of a Lifetime	136
Chill	139
7:30 A.M.	140
Least Common Denominator	141
Shoreline Watercolors	142

CONTENTS

The First Two Opportunities of a Day	143
Without a Choice in the Matter	146
Hypothetical Omniscience	149
Approval Rating	151
Inch and a Half Rain	152
Also with You	153
Twice	154
Beyond Reason	155
Light of Day	156
Divergent Aftermath	157
July 4	158
Night Light	159
Tangible Image of an Unknown Thought	160
Bookending an Extraordinary Interim	161
Lost Welcome	162
Think Before Taking Over a Large Yard	163
Rusty	174
Smile at Life	175
Ode to a Forthcoming Doctoral Dissertation	176
Upon Reflection	177
1956	179
A Typical Day	185
Birds of a Feather	188
Charity Begins at Home	191
Instant Rebate	193
Bee	198
Campaign Trail	199
Get Up	200
Four Crayons, Ten Minutes	201
Departure	202
About the Author	203

Premise

Poetry is not as much about something,
As it is a glimpse into it.

Transitory Advantage

Without exaggerated toe or heel pressure,
A straight line of impressions in dry sand,
Planted in long strides
By large athletic shoes with deep-cut waffle soles,
Paced off an uninterrupted destination.

Fainter soles of two small feet,
Striving to keep up,
Skipped or ran
With stronger toe pressure here,
Skidding heel pressure there.

The variable-length zigzag strides,
Sometimes beside, sometimes behind,
Sometimes intersecting themselves,
Occasionally obliterated the center
Of a deep-cut waffle print.

Saturday Morning

Several times I have seen them,
A single file like large ants,
Pedaling along the ridgetop highway,
Aggressively challenging
The passing stream of traffic
To which, more likely than not,
They give comeuppance
At the next traffic light.

Heads forward and slightly down,
They stay in line, pedal in unison,
And communicate with nuanced body language.
Occasionally one breaks out,
Like the third rider this morning,
Who pulled abreast of the second.
Either of them could have passed again and seized the lead,
But neither did.

They are a stereotypic unit
With perforated aerodynamic helmets,
Twenty-nine-inch-waist Lycra skins,
And bulging gastrocnemius muscles,
Who gather machismo bragging rights
For Monday-through-Friday recollections
Of strenuous, exceptional speed
Along peripheral boundaries of open roads.

Although all sorts of people ride bicycles,
I think of serious tandem cycling
As a predominately male sport
—modern cowboys heading up and moving out.
It was fittingly appropriate to learn
The riders on the ridge this morning
Were led by a female preschool teacher
Whose left leg is a prosthesis.

Severance

He was her second husband.
They were twenty-one when they married.
Often he found himself turning his ring with his thumb,
Absently mining its joy and polishing its luster.

When he washed his hands,
The ring got special suds and rinsing.
It glistened in clear water
And gleamed in sunlight.

Four years into marriage,
He was finishing graduate school and working part-time.
She had a full-time job and was adamant that she did not want a child
Before they could move from their small apartment into a home of their own.

Days went by as though the topic had been a casual chat.
Nights were as erotic as ever.
Perhaps there was another reason
She was extremely careful not to conceive.

He was offered a California job at graduation.
They discussed her employment options also.
She seemed all right with the decision, not terribly enthusiastic, but all right.
Yet there was an infinitesimally slight change in the way she acted.

His new company paid their relocation expenses,
Provided a temporary apartment with a balcony and ocean view,
And arranged several job interviews for her.
They were on the verge of reaping the American dream.
Because, as she told him, it had happened so fast,
Two weeks after they moved in,
She wanted to make a trip back to surprise her father on his birthday,
And deferred committing to a new job until she returned.

Although disappointed, he said he understood.
He bought her a seven-day round-trip plane ticket.

They had a wonderful dinner, laughed, talked about buying more furniture,
And had the most tender lovemaking he could remember.

She flew out at dawn.
As he watched the plane make a wide arc over the ocean,
It slowly climbed high into the blue and disappeared.
Musing in the void, he drove slower than usual to work.

A little after noon, she called to tell him she had landed.
That night they talked again about her day,
Things like food, the weather, and that she was tired.
Then he said, "I love you," and she bid him good night.

The next day he called to tell her good morning.
Her mother said she was still asleep.
Odd, he thought, *it is two hours later there than here.*
His day was full of meetings, and it was evening before he could call again.

After scarcely a word about her dad, she talked about herself.
The conversation was pleasant, loquacious, and perfunctory.
He tried hard to make an end that said *I love you,*
And could only bring himself to say, "Good night . . . sleep well."

He did not call her the next day until evening.
He asked how she was and told her he missed her terribly.
So as not to interfere with the last two days of her stay,
Could *she* call *him* next time?

The following twenty-four hours gathered anxiety as the day progressed.
She did not call in the morning, but he did not expect her to wake him up.
Throughout the day she was probably squeezing in last-minute errands.
After dinner the phone was quiet until he finally went to bed at eleven o'clock.

Next morning he anguished over what to do.
Should he call her and say *good morning* as though nothing had happened?
Should he bide his time and wait for her to call him and, hopefully, apologize?

He decided to send her a text message: *How are you doing?*

The response was so quick he still had the cell phone in his hand.
I am not coming back, I filed for divorce yesterday.
He was numb, went to work and told no one.
Friday and throughout the weekend, he continuously asked himself, *Why?*

Monday a sheriff's deputy served the petition,
And twenty days of negotiations required by law began.
All he owned was their old furniture, his clothes, and college debt.
He did not contest the divorce; in a blur of three months it was over.

He removed his gold band the day he was served the petition.
Reluctant and embarrassed, he forced himself to tell people she had gone.
He grew weary wondering *why*.
Then one day he came upon an interesting finding.

The worst storms at sea churn no more than 300 feet of water below.
The next Sunday morning he caught the Catalina Ferry out of Dana Point,
Dropped the gold wedding band overboard into 400 feet of water,
And it was gone . . . gone . . . taking the need for reason with it.

About Face

1

The eighteen-month-old spelunker crawled into the imaginary cave behind the sofa.
Before reaching the other side,
He came upon a lamp cord and attempted to pull it from the socket.
It would not budge.
Doing what eighteen-month-olds do,
He brought it to his mouth.
As he sucked and slobbered,
It felt good on his gums where new molars were trying to erupt.
He chewed,
It felt even better,
Especially when he clenched hard.
He began to gnaw with his canines,
Making resolute progress into the new crevice he was creating.
Then his mouth exploded.
His mother and father,
A mere cushion-thickness away,
Winced, jerked, and flung the divan from the wall.
They beheld a tongue without a tip,
And corners of his mouth splayed open an inch on both sides.
The charred flesh hardly bled at all.
Agony that poured from his body
Coalesced with their torrents of throbbing fear.
They grieved for years afterward,
But never allowed him to know their pervasive guilt
Or hear the devastating words they intended to carry to their graves:
"If only."
They loved him into manhood with singleness of heart,
And he, beyond awareness,
Redeemed their sorrow by discovering happiness each day.
He worked in his dad's restaurant,
Became a first-responder emergency medical technician,

And thrived as an amateur boxer.
After a few moments of introductory conversation,
Few people gave a second thought to his lisp or quirky smile.
He kissed many women,
And at his wedding,
His father made a simple toast:
"To miracles!"

2

Dry wind and more than a week of ninety-degree days
Had ripened the winter wheat to perfection.
The bumper crop was the best in years.
Sunup until well into the night,
Five thousand competing custom cutter crews
Rolled over one field after another
To earn a year's income in five months.
On their way from Texas to North Dakota,
They were less than halfway there.

The family rig consisted of a combine, grain truck, pickup, and camping trailer.
Though illegal, a thirteen-year-old boy's contribution was essential.
He drove the grain truck back and forth from field to elevator.

My parents were visiting my aunt at the country doctor's hospital.
The dim white hall with a dull, muddy-green linoleum floor
Was cluttered with muslin screens, a gurney,
And sinister-looking medical equipment.
I fidgeted in one of the half dozen wooden chairs against the front window.
Wall-mounted fans stirred the hot air with ether fumes.
Between where I sat and the operating room at the other end of the building,
Unknown things, perhaps terrible things,
Were happening to people in rooms on both sides of the corridor.
I wished my folks would come out.
I wanted to leave.

A horn approached from somewhere.
It wasn't an ambulance.
HONK, HONK, HONK . . . HONK, HONK!
An old pickup rounded the dusty corner a block away
And skidded to a halt at the front door of the small waiting room.
Two men in grimy bib overalls jumped out, yelling for help.
One carried a boy like a soldier retrieving a fallen comrade from a battlefield.
A nurse in a starched white uniform raced from a patient's room down the hall.
The boy was burned brilliant red
From where there had been hair on the top of his head
To midway down his small naked chest.
He was shaking and heaving for breath.
I could not understand why he was not screaming or crying.
Another nurse came from somewhere.
She guided all of them into the room beside where I sat.
No one thought to close the wide door.
One of the nurses gave the boy a shot
While the other began smearing him with a clear jelly or grease.
He shuddered and moaned
But did not recoil or scream.
I had trouble looking away as my parents guided me out the same door
Through which the men had brought the boy into the hospital.
"What happened to him?" I said.

I did not get an answer until a year later
When we returned to see my aunt again;
Fortunately, not in the hospital.
She said the boy's grain truck stalled because of a vapor lock.
He had removed the air cleaner, blown out the carburetor,
And was pouring gasoline into the carburetor's throat when it exploded.
His mother stayed with him in the hospital
While the rest of the family continued the harvest.

Years passed before I learned more.
The boy went back to the rig.

Eventually his father could no longer stand the grind,
And the boy, then a man, and his brother-in-law took over the business.
They have not missed a harvest in forty years.
For lack of enough money or insurance,
Or perhaps because he had already endured enough pain,
Or perhaps because he was skeptical of what could be done,
He did not have skin grafts or scar revisions.
He has facial expression on the right side.
On the left side, his face and neck look like an ungauzed mummy.
Now that his mother is gone,
His sister is the closest female in his life.
Hundreds of farm families, elevator operators, and small-town folks
From Texas to the Canadian border
Know him by name and look forward to seeing him each year.
No one has ever known him to ignore a child,
Fail to shake a farmer's hand,
Or not say "thank you" for the opportunity to cut the largest—or the smallest—field.
Farmers' wives know his favorite meal is hot, crispy, pan-fried chicken,
Mashed potatoes with extra gravy,
Banana cream pie,
And lots of ice-cold tea.
He remembers stories people tell him,
And somehow keeps them straight to follow up next time around.
None of the people he serves
Would ever dream of letting another crew cut their wheat,
Nor does he think of them any other way than as his family.

3

Four-thirty a.m. on a Wednesday,
The airport security queue was already doubling on itself.
The TSA agent exhorted people to be prepared for the "Next Person in Line" signal.
Thereafter, grabbing possessions and redressing themselves,
Everybody walked as fast as they could both on and off the moving walkways.

Gate seating was full.
People were standing.
Students were spread around the floors tethered to electrical outlets.
Generation Xers in business attire
Simultaneously juggled open laptops,
Cell phones with or without earbuds,
And venti-size cups of Starbucks coffee.
Garbled announcements from every gate overlapped so much
That even with vigilance, comprehension was nearly impossible.
Video wall monitors and the formation and migration of crowd clusters
Were the best gauges of progress toward boarding a flight.

A boy, three or four years old,
Played with small cars at his mother's feet.
Facing him on the opposite side of the narrow line of chairs
Sat an unrecognizable person.
Horribly disfigured beyond comprehension, with burn scars from head to toe,
It had no hair, no ears, no nose.
Its hands ended in contracted partial fingers with no nails.
Below its Bermuda shorts,
One leg was prosthetic,
The other was a patchwork of skin that resembled oak tree bark.
Judging by the form of its torso,
This person was once a muscular young man.
People stole furtive glances at him, then averted their eyes.
Everyone, that is, but the small boy.
He looked up at the man and said, "Do you want to play cars?"
If eyes had not seen the person,
And only sound was used to envision him,
It would have been the strong, clear, friendly voice of a nice man.
He said, "Sure!"
Although he could not reach the floor to hold a car,
The two of them enjoyed the imaginary game.
Together they shared the narration,
And the boy was the animation.
He looked back and forth between the man and the cars,
Smiling and laughing, totally engaged.

When their flight was called,
The boy's mother brought him in tow and started to leave.
The boy hesitated a moment and turned to the man.
"Here, you need one too," he said,
And placed one of his cars in the man's pocket.
The burned man was slow and let others go in front of him.
He was one of the last to board the aircraft,
And sat at the rear of the plane.
There was takeoff,
A smooth two-and-a-half-hour flight,
Then touchdown and taxiing to the gate.
The seat-belt sign was turned off,
But the exit door was not yet open.
In collective urgency to deplane,
People rose from their seats,
Flooded the aisle,
And began opening overhead bins.
Unexpectedly, the aircraft went dark and a voice on the speakers said,
"This is your captain. Everybody please be seated."
A rumble of discontentment spread throughout the plane.
"What's going on?" was the predominant comment.
"Ladies and gentlemen, we have a great honor.
Traveling with us today is one of America's finest,
A soldier who lives for all of us.
He is returning home from Iraq.
Please let Marine Lance Corporal Benjamin Vasquez
Lead us off the aircraft."
People instantly cleared the aisle, falling back into their seats.
The plane erupted into applause, whistles, and cheers.
Lance Corporal Benjamin Vasquez slowly made his way up the aisle.
There was not enough of his face left to smile or shed a tear,
But his fellow passengers did both for him.
All the way to the front he nodded his head up and down
And haltingly raised his right arm.
In his pocket he carried a small car.
Somewhere on the plane was the boy who had given it to him
When all the people now applauding
Had looked the other way.

Perseverance

Like gray chocolate,
Fog flows over the backside ridge
And pours cold, thick batter into the canyon below.
Entering here on the opposite side
Is like descending into a smoldering ocean
That encapsulates phantom depth in all directions.
I turn up my collar
And, for sure-footedness,
Pay close attention to the ground directly ahead.

Start to finish,
Awareness that something out there
Could be a threat,
Or merely minding its own business,
Reinforces an acute vigilance.
Other than to survey the surroundings,
Stopping is not an option.
As long as going back is possible,
Fog parts the way equally well ahead.

How Many for How Much

You, Oh Land,
Wild, free, and old,
And we,
Incipient, needy, and transient,
Are in this realm together,
Not a realm of our own invitations,
But from creation beyond understanding.

You here, and here will be,
And we, imbued with need to find a way
To live in communities
And perpetuate ourselves,
Venture like ants into wilderness,
Filing in line to and from our nests
In meandering spoke-like columns.

In the macrocosm of collective purpose,
For love or primal satisfaction
—reasons known only in each of seven billion hearts—
As our numbers increase exponentially,
Our need and action
Appropriate you
Into the critical mass.

Provoked by the density,
We pursue light and fresh air,
And wonder where it goes
From afternoons we rest on a rock,
Or picnic in a meadow,
Or walk in woods
Among fallen trees and songbirds in high boughs.

As we build
150-, 300-, 800-, 3,000-, 15,000-square-foot living spaces
Day in and out,
Fewer and fewer of us make the time

To venture beyond the expanding fringes of urbanization.
Although we cannot reclaim the way you were before,
You do your best to help us where we are.

Knowing We Don't

Where snow does not come in winter
   stands a lone sycamore tree,
   descendent of a hundred-million-year-old family,
   sustained,
   as far as anyone knows,
   without awareness of itself in the universe.

I look at the night sky above it
   in awe of eternity,
   unable to grasp more
   than my personal ancestry,
   receding at most
   no more than a century or two.

Theoretically, a genetic twist traces back
   to a primordial cell
   in a molecule of water
   from which a code
   has linked all living things
   since the beginning.

From before the beginning,
   streams of photons
   have winnowed through interstellar space
   and presumably will go on forever
   until they collide
   with a critical mass of molecules or black hole energy.

Scientists speculate the naked eye can distinguish
   forty thousand separate points of starlight photons
   that manage to reach the molecules of our retinas,
   attesting infinitesimal participation
   in the vast cosmos,
   with no idea of the implications.

Economics Lesson

Opal started to move
Twenty years after her husband died.
She sold her home
And rented a high-rise apartment.

Two years was enough time
To enjoy the panoramic view of Lake Michigan through casement windows.
She wanted to be back outside
To read, watch songbirds, and enjoy coffee and newspapers.

Since Milwaukee summers were short and there were mosquitos,
Movers came and transported her things
Back to the Kansas prairie town where she had spent her youth
And early married years before WWII whisked them off to Maryland.

The rented townhome had an enclosed garden
With a brick patio beneath an apple tree.
It came with wonderful wrought iron furniture,
To which she applied a fresh coat of white paint.

Five Julys later the landlord sold the house
On one of the hottest days of the year.
Within a month the rent increased fifty percent,
And the new owner appropriated the wrought iron furniture for himself.

Naïvely remembering nothing but cool summers,
She called movers to return her things to a Milwaukee duplex
Where she shared the neighbor's wicker furniture
On a front porch without privacy.

The second winter, she slipped on ice as she mounted the steps.
Elbow surgery that required several weeks' convalescence
Convinced her not to risk a recurrence,
So she called movers again to return her things to Kansas.

Eighty years old, a lifetime U.S. government pension, an annuity,
And certificates of deposit she rolled over rather than spend

Were not compelling enough reasons
To buy nice furniture for someone else's property.

Bright red geraniums filled the two-foot-high planter
Surrounding her patio facing the street.
She bought two cheap, folding lawn chairs
And took them inside at night to prevent theft.

When seat-webbing failed on the one facing east,
She did not replace it.
She simply changed the position of the other chair twice a day
Until she moved across town for a better view.

Many warm days found her on the balcony outside her new living room
Sitting on a wooden chair she took back and forth from the kitchen table.
Once in a while she invited friends for an alfresco lunch
Served on a folding card table covered with a tablecloth.

At ninety, she moved the last time,
Transitioning from independent living in a studio
To assisted living in a bedroom of her own,
To nursing care in a bed separated by a curtain from someone else.

Without hope of a patio ever again,
Her peripatetic clock had stopped.
She died and left her money to a niece
Who spent it vacationing domestically and abroad.

In retrospect,
A mobile home would have been a good investment;
And since she couldn't take her money with her when she died,
She might as well have enjoyed sitting on some of it before she did.

The Dachshund and the Greyhound

A man in a light jacket,
With a greyhound close at hand on a leash,
Zigzagged to avoid puddles.
All the lawns were still brown.
Lingering snow mounds here and there
Trickled seepage into mud in the road.
A few crocuses that matched the hazy blue sky
Indicated that winter thaw was almost complete
And it was time to avail the vigor of spring.

Across the street,
A girl got out of a car
And traversed the yard to the front porch.
When a boy swung open the screen door to greet her,
A light-brown dachshund
Rushed out between their feet
And began running circles in the yard.
The girl went on inside,
Leaving the boy to call the dog back.

There was no response.
He said something over his shoulder into the house,
And pointed toward the greyhound
Walking dutifully beside his master on the other side of the street.
The words exchanged were something to the effect,
"That is the skinniest dog I have ever seen."
Little did they know he was ninety pounds of solid muscle,
Retired from three years' racing
Because he did not run faster than thirty miles an hour.

Being the sight hound he was,
The greyhound would not take his eyes off the dachshund.
Its stubby little legs swung back and forth at lightning speed,
Yet it did not quickly go anywhere.
The greyhound seemed more than grateful

To be dawdling along on his long broomsticks.
If dog thoughts could be known,
He was perhaps thinking,
That guy stayed way too long at the track!

Mother Knew

Autumns when orchards sold apples by the bushel,
Drops and culls not crushed for cider
Were offered by the peck at half price.
She put them up as apple butter in wide-mouth mason jars.

Throughout winter,
On cold snowy mornings when my fingers were crossed
That school would be called off,
Before donning rubber boots,
A hand-knitted scarf,
A scratchy wool mackinaw,
And mittens linked with a string inside the back
Between one sleeve and the other,
Apple butter spread on warm toast
Was so good,
That a second piece dispelled my reluctance to go.

Trekking out into the cold school day
Seemed like Saturday.

Ever the Boy Who Dreamed Such a Dream

Behind the duplex,
Converted at the start of World War II into four apartments,
Industrial-frame chicken-wire glass windows
Fronted the terra-cotta-tile flat-roof garage.
On the alley side,
Bifold doors jerked in ratchets
When tugged along the rusted overhead track.
A raised, concrete threshold demarcated
The unpaved inside from the unpaved alley.

In this blue-collar neighborhood,
Vandalism was unheard of.
Even in pitch blackness,
With electric lights neither inside nor outside,
A blizzard forecast was the only motivation for closing any of the four stalls.
For some reason,
Perhaps it was the pungency of the old, raw wood beams and partitions,
Wasps and birds found it better elsewhere,
And feral cats did not use the floor.

Two years after the war,
When the boy was seven,
His father drove a company car he parked on the front street.
His mother did not drive.
She walked to neighborhood stores
Or rode the bus downtown.
One day his father bought a tan 1936 Plymouth sedan
—a spare car he called it, at a good price—
And put it in the garage.

Some Sundays after fried chicken or pot roast,
Father, Mother, and he took the Plymouth for rides
Through new subdivisions, out to the airport,
And down the main street into the heart of town.
Although it was older than he was,

And many people in the neighborhood
Owned newer Chevys or Fords,
To him, it was the best car in the world
—he was a *Plymouth man.*

The chrome three-masted clipper ship hood ornament,
Emblem of the slogan *Sailing Along,*
Conveyed it all.
He pretended President Truman himself
Would step onto the running board,
Enter the rear-hinged back door using the upholstered grab strap,
Sit on the soft wool seat with a center armrest,
Slide the rear side window open for air,
And tell his chauffeur where he wanted to go.

He was the President's chauffeur.
But first, just like they did at Clark's filling station,
He lifted the driver's side of the gull-wing hood
And pretended to pull the oil stick,
Check the wide white sidewall tires for enough air,
Run a chamois through the wringer,
Wash the windows,
And brush out the floors with a whisk broom.
Before he got back inside, he rolled down all four side windows.

Once behind the three-spoke steering wheel,
He cranked the cowl ventilator up and the windshield out,
Pulled the choke lever halfway,
Turned the imaginary ignition key,
And depressed the starter pedal.
All gauges on the large, round dashboard dial started moving:
Gas, oil pressure, engine temperature, and battery were normal.
The choke, manual throttle, and headlight knobs were pushed in.
The long speedometer needle was ready to leave its peg.

Squeezing the emergency brake handle and pushing it forward,
He disengaged the clutch,
Palmed the floor-shift lever side to side

A couple of times in the middle of the *H*,
Then pushed it into the upper-left position,
Looked back over both shoulders,
Gave it some gas,
Slowly let the clutch out,
And backed into the alley.

Clutch in,
Brake pedal in,
Shift straight down to the lower left of the H,
Turn the wheels,
Brake pedal out,
Add some gas and let the clutch out slowly.
Down the alley he went
With the purr of his mother's treadle sewing machine,
Taking President Truman for a ride.

Driving only in his mind,
Glancing at the backseat in the rearview mirror,
He dreamed of the day he would be fourteen
And could get a learner's permit.
Sixty-six years later, backing out of his attached double garage,
He looked at the screen of his rearview camera
And was taken back for a moment
To the day he returned from school
And the Plymouth was gone.
Behind the two-story duplex
He had driven a car that never moved,
Into a world never the same again:
An interstate highway system
Accommodating 250 million vehicles,
Thirty-two lanes of traffic at four-way intersections,
Parking lots the size of small farms,
And self-driving concept cars—
All within his lifetime.

Second-Grade Soul

Rodney was the poorest kid in second grade.
He had unkempt, home-cut hair.
His clothes,
Worn and wrinkled,
More likely than not
Had come from the Salvation Army.
His belt was too long,
His mackinaw too small,
His shirts sometimes lacked buttons.

In class,
He never raised his hand to offer an answer,
Yet always had one if Miss Heckert called on him.
His classmates,
Themselves from modest means,
Would have paid special attention
To avoid a poor kid who was a bully,
But they mostly ignored
The quiet kid with holes in his shoes.

Similarly,
Second graders don't intuitively think much
About other kids being lonely,
They are just aware
Lonely kids don't have friends.
Rodney played at recess,
But when the 3:30 bell signaled school was out,
He was gone.
No one went to his house;
He never had homemade cookies and milk
At anyone else's.

One day someone asked about his mother.
After uncomfortable hesitation,
He said, "She's sick."

Silence followed.
No one asked more,
Though momentarily they thought of Donald,
Whose mother, brother, and sister
Were killed a few months earlier
By a train hitting their car.
When Donald returned to class,
It somehow seemed unsafe to be near him.
By association,
Fate of an ordinary day
Might go horribly wrong again.

It didn't,
And the apprehension passed.
Thoughts of the absence of a mother,
Or feminine surrogate of a mother,
Receded like memory of a dream
About a gloomy day in someone else's house.
Donald was Donald again.

Rodney, on the other hand,
Neither a victim of sudden tragedy nor neglect,
Was simply a child of hardship.

On a day when Miss Heckert
Asked her students to bring something to class to talk about,
Rodney brought a tarnished old alto saxophone.
"This is my dad's."
Stroking the instrument,
He explained the neck, the body,
The keys, the rods, the pads, the thumb rest, the cork,
And how to wet and blow the mouthpiece.

He closed his eyes,
Lifted the instrument to his lips,
And blew amazing, loud, sweet music.
Miss Heckert was aghast
And compelled to interrupt,

But she didn't.
Sound poured through the closed door into the hall.
Miss Bond and Miss Taylor
Rushed from their adjoining classrooms.
Miss Watkins, the principal,
Was close behind.
Miss Heckert's students gaped in disbelief.
Rodney didn't notice.
His eyes still closed,
At one with his instrument,
Nodding slowly forward and back,
Like water from an artesian well into a community font,
Music poured from him,
Sound over sound,
Until he abruptly realized
Transcendence of his core into the nether realm
Had left his body in reality.

He stopped mid-echo of a note.
His classmates,
Still frozen in silence,
Moved only their eyes
Between him and Miss Heckert.
Miss Watkins started an applause
That ended the anxious moment.
Rodney was horrified.
Then, looking down,
He started to smile.

The boy no one could remember smiling before
Was an only child
Whose mother was in a tuberculosis sanatorium.
His father was a janitor in an old commercial building
At the fringe of downtown.
In a corner of basement lodgings,
Where in cold weather they slept beside the boiler,
After the business closed and was clean,

His dad taught him to play the saxophone.
He gave him ear cotton and earmuffs,
And told him to imagine
He was standing on the rim of the Grand Canyon at midnight,
Playing to the Milky Way.

Four and a Half Billion Years and Counting

Glimpse the concentric ripples
From the ping of a single drop of water in a teacup.
Observe the swirl
From the tremolo of water cascading tier to tier in a garden fountain.
Behold the torrent
From the Colorado River roaring through Hoover Dam.

Water,
No matter where it falls,
Irrespective of how quiet or loud,
Makes not a sound
As it evaporates over and over back into the air,
One ocean after another.

An Opportunity Prayer

Thank you, God, for gravity and friction:

Gravity that holds everything together,
Terrestrial and celestial,
In affinity;

Friction that allows movement
By molecules pressing against one another
Without disintegration.

The paths along which we go are there
Because of firmness on which to place our feet
And traction with which to find our way.

Playing Logical God with a Nuclear Collider

Mathematicians and physicists
Probe to understand energy for what it is;
The rest of us
Respect it for what it does.

The first rocks,
Brewed of energy in a cosmic crucible,
Became matter,
Forever lasting in three of many forms:

    Water,
    The great magician
    That cycles through ice-stone
    And blows away in wind.

    Fire,
    Blaze,
    Ember, and ash
    That returns in water to rock.

    And life,
    That somehow began in water,
    Flourishes forward
    And leaves behind a trail of itself in coal, oil, and fossils.

In 2013
Enormous energy
Revealed *Higgs Boson*
Is not the name of God.

In vain to understand *why*,
We press on
In search of *how*
Creation occurred.

A strange courier,
The one left in Pandora's box,

Hope,
Leads us to discover

Creation is not an end time
Available to start over.
It is not past tense.
It is now.

Sprinklers that Run in the Rain

A sprinkler running in the rain
Is like a match burning in a forest fire,
A fan blowing in a wind,
A man thinking in a bar,
An athlete making twenty million dollars on a sport,
And a hundred million dollars on endorsements.

January Night

Two hundred miles below the Arctic Circle,
Clothed in down-filled parkas with ruffs zipped into peepholes,
Nylon pants over flannel-lined jeans over thermal underwear,
Double gloves, cotton booties inside wool socks, and high-top thermal boots,
We ventured into the forty-degree-below-zero cold.

Never without companionship,
Always in groups of two or three,
We trudged through knee-deep snow
That swallowed conversation
And did not echo back.

In the middle of the vast valley
We navigated on a dark, far-distant cabin,
Polaris in the north sky,
And footprints a moose or caribou
Had pawed through the snow.

Without a moon,
The clear heaven beckoned,
LOOK UP, LOOK UP,
At pastel energy swirling through the starlight
Like God's omnipotent breath
Cascading over an invisible boulder field.

Craning backward to see directly overhead
While struggling not to pitch over,
We turned 360 degrees again and again.
Until our necks could no longer endure the pain,
And our gazes lowered to the tundra.

The seductive cold tugged like a sorcerer's chain,
Enchanting us from exerting effort to turn back through the deep holes
Our steps had made getting there.
It was prudence, not desire,
That brought us home.

Yesterday, Today, Tomorrow

I am late to the room
To become a vocational poet,
So in avocation I write from experiences
Prodding me for interpretation
To a new age,
Of a past
Not that long ago,
Bridging into a future
Not that far away,
When there may be value
In knowing something firsthand,
Otherwise lost.

In the Course of a Business Day

The mountains that surround this valley
Once separated it from the outside world by several days' journey.
People hungered for any morsel of information brought overland on a horse.
Everywhere today, around-the-globe access to reality
Is as easy as tapping the face of a cell phone,
Or speaking to its search engine
As though it were a person.

But like the old days,
In the constraint of many airline cabins between takeoff and landing,
No matter how urgent the need to know,
No matter how eager the need for reinvolvement
In things done and left undone,
Suspended connection with the outside world
Is imposed without an option.

Here beneath the plane,
As news is coming in,
It sweeps empathy across my day.
An hour ago on the other side of the world,
In a valley probably not much different from where I stand,
Aircraft launched rockets annihilating popular resistance to a totalitarian regime,
And left a society in the rubble and blood of its own hands.

Above me, the falling pitch of the aircraft engines signals a different outcome.
Its payload of morning passengers
Is moving toward a city sixty miles away.
Their day that began at 4:30 this morning
Is focused on the next eight to twelve hours.
Most of the people are working the last few moments
Until a flight attendant will shut them down.

Minutes later the first words into their cell phones will be,
"I have landed."

They will scramble through the cabin door and down a crowded gangway,
Merge with hundreds more passengers like themselves
Into confluent swirling like starlings in a high wind.
With slight notice they will pass breaking news on numerous television screens
Before reaching busy loading zones to more important locations.

Reentry

A sweep of synchronous limbs
Undulates like a Chinese New Year dragon
Kicking up spurts of corn snow
With its piercing claws.

Returning from their last engagement with the mountain for a year,
The squadron's speed exceeds the tailwind
That washes across their landing strip below
And shears pillows of smoke from the lodge's chimney.

At the last possible moment
Their edges scrape to abrupt stops at the rack.
They whip off their balaclavas
And shout joyous vapor clouds at one another.

Tomorrow they will all depart at dawn
Into an unsettling day
During which *run* changes from a recreational noun
Into a workplace verb.

Bittersweet Finality

There was not a time I jumped up from play,
Gathered my toys, every last one,
And hauled them out to the curb for the Salvation Army truck to take away.
No, it did not happen that way.

I got rid of some for no particular reason.
But the toys I speak of were my favorites,
Until they found themselves at the bottom of the toy box more and more.
Each time I cleaned it out, there were not as many to put back.

A few at a time,
That's how they disappeared.
I don't remember the first to go, or the last.
I simply opened the lid one day and the box was empty.

The boy standing there,
Who did not yet know he was a man,
Abruptly realized he could not go back.
It was too late.

School Shoes

August was the last month to play outside after dark.
Mosquito bites were doctored with Mercurochrome,
Thicker-than-usual bathtub rings had to be scrubbed with Bab-O,
And it was time to get a new pair of school shoes.

The most popular boy's style was a brown oxford
With holes punched in the overlaid toecap,
Wide, flat cotton laces and rubber or leather heels.
Rubber was a poor choice because it left black marks on linoleum floors.

The Saturday destination was a big event.
You took a number from a ticket machine,
And while you waited beneath the entrance awning,
Kids came out smiling with their new shoes.

When it was your turn,
You sat down in front of an inclined stool,
Took off one shoe, pulled up your sock,
And put your foot on a sizing device the salesman called *The Brannock*.

He adjusted the sides to the width of your foot,
Pushed your big toe down on the scale,
Took the measurements,
And brought out two boxes.

He opened the measured-size box first,
Crinkled back the tissue paper,
Pulled the shoe tongue up, stretched the sides out,
And scooped your foot in with his shoehorn.

After lacing the eyelets and tying the knot with a flourish, he said,
    "Okay, step down.
      This may be a little tight, but it will stretch;
        . . . walk over to the mirror and back."

Maybe it was not tight, but it was stiff.
He pushed your big toe with the ball of his thumb,

Said to your mother, "Feel this?"
She did, and nodded her head yes.

"How does it feel to you, young man?"
When you said nothing because you did not know what to say,
The salesman continued,
"Let's try the bigger size on your other foot."

It felt better,
But he put his finger into the space at the heel and said,
"This will slip and wear a hole in your sock."
You still did not know what to say.

You looked at your parents,
You looked at the salesman,
You looked at your two feet,
And you asked your parents for advice.

Before they could answer,
The salesman said,
"Walk around some more,
Then let's see how they do."

It was time for the magic shoe-fitting fluoroscope.
Burkabees was the only shoe store in town that had one;
It was why people went there.
The machine made sure you got exactly the right size.

You slid your feet into the mouse hole at the bottom.
You, your mom or dad, and the salesman
Looked into the three viewers,
And the salesman made a pitch for the first shoes he brought out.

You did not know until later what your dad was thinking:
Is the salesman trying to sell us the smaller shoes
Because they will be outgrown faster and he can sell another pair sooner,
Or are they really the right size for healthy feet?

For no reason other than the fluoroscope was irrefutable,
You went home with the smaller shoes,

And broke them in a week before school started.
Sure enough, they stretched just like the salesman said they would.

The four rules for school shoes were:

(1) When you put them on,
Don't force or wiggle your feet in.
Unlace the strings and raise the tongues,
Otherwise, you will mash down the counters.

(2) Never play in them after school.
Take them off as soon as you get home, but not before,
Because you might lose them,
Or someone might tie them together and throw them in a tree.

(3) Polish them every Saturday morning,
And let them air out the rest of the day
So they will be ready for Sunday
And not stink.

(4) Never, never, never get them wet,
Because if you do,
They will squeak,
And if they squeak, you will have to wear them anyway.

George Gow at 800 on the Philco dial
Helped out in that regard.
If he said it would rain or snow,
You took galoshes to school even if the sun was shining.

Sometime mid–school year
The heels had become round and the soles thin.
The shoe shop replaced them both,
And buffed the leather tops like new.

When summer arrived, it was bare feet and sneakers time.
The brown oxfords had served their purpose.
To the shoe salesman's credit, or perhaps his fluoroscope's,
They had been the right size throughout the entire second grade.

Barefoot Girl in a Calico Dress

Between 1831–37 the U.S. Government relocated the Choctaw and Chickasaw Nations from Mississippi to Oklahoma over the Trail of Tears.

1902.

Nine hundred acres of the reservation
Were expropriated back for white settlers,
Elva Lea was two years old,
A railway spur was built to the main line,
A hatchet and a horseshoe, for peace and good luck,
Were buried within a new concrete bridge across Rock Creek,
And a public park was constructed to encourage harmony among people thereabouts.

1907.

Oklahoma became a state one month after Elva Lea turned seven.
With a tinge of Native American beauty and raven black hair,
She was next to the youngest of three girls and a boy.
Void of knowledge of any place but the tiny town of Springwater,
The small bedroom she shared with her two sisters,
An outhouse privy,
And kerosene lamps,
She played long days in red dirt
Bathed away at night in a washtub
Of hand-pumped water
Heated on a woodstove in the kitchen.

1909.

Multiplication, cursive, and the Oregon Trail
Were perhaps important at school,
But essential education
Was learning to cook and sew with her mother and sisters,
Avoiding snakes, especially in the chicken coop and the garden,
Hurling a pail of water from the back porch without getting wet,
And pinning laundry straight and tight on the clothesline.

Her brother, Leverett,
Second oldest of the siblings,
Taught her how to build a campfire,
Tie knots,
And whistle with two fingers.

Papa was a railroad lineman,
Often gone days at a time.
Cold winter nights when he was home,
After supper in dim lamplight beside the potbelly stove,
The family shared conversation and stories.
They sang while Papa played the old upright piano by ear
. . . and they laughed a lot.

That Christmas,
Remembered above all others,
They strung three popcorn strands and paired off into teams:
Papa and Leverett,
Elva Lea's mother and older sister, Mattie,
And she and her younger sister, Plassee.
Through clenched teeth clamped on the taut string,
Papa said, "Go!"
Without touching the string with their hands,
Everyone gobbled popcorn as fast as they could toward the middle.
Amid the energy
Much popcorn was spit,
Nobody choked,
Papa and Leverett won.

Spring came.
Papa was on a train up north.
Gathering clouds in the southwest
Coalesced beneath the late-afternoon sun.
A skittish breeze poking here and there
Unsettled the chickens.
Soon the advancing front
Sprouted angry whorls resembling large brown soap bubbles.
Its leading edge drug darkness over the house.

Without a storm cellar to rush to,
Small flickers and low, distant rumbles
Drew them to the porch to watch.
When the breeze gusted and then abruptly stopped dead-still,
They hurried back inside.
It was calm but a moment before torrential rain lashed upon the land
And sheeted the windows in waves.
Blue-white lightning flashing through the lace curtains
Cast spectral images over everything.
Thunder rattled the windows like artillery.
Hail hammered the tin roof.
Elva Lea knew the storm would soon take the house
And all of them with it.

In the corner farthest from the windows,
She and her sisters, wrapped in a quilt,
Cowered beside their mother on the daybed.
Leverett, remembering Papa taught him that will is a strong courage,
Sat silently beside them on the floor,
His back stiffly braced against the bed.
Eventually the fury receded,
The parlor was pitch-black,
And the girls fell asleep in their mother's arms.

Another night three months later,
Summer had come.
In the clear darkness abundant with fireflies,
Papa was home.
The family sat on the front porch
And mused that a clear night sky is the only proof of eternity
Humans can know for sure.
They talked of the baby soon to arrive.
Papa went into the house and returned with the family Bible.
He lit the lantern
And read the Sermon on the Mount to them.

A few days later,
The same lantern hung on a nail above the front step.

The children waited.
Papa summoned Leverett to get help.
Two neighbor women came without a doctor.
The dog howled on and off throughout the night.
By morning,
Mary Opal was born,
And her mother was dead.
Elva Lea was eight years old.
Plassee was five.

Because Papa had no other recourse
Than to return to the railroad to keep food on the table,
Mattie and Leverett became the effective parents.
She was sixteen and quit school
To take care of the baby, the laundry, and the meals.
Elva Lea and Plassee got themselves ready for school
And, miraculously, never missed a day of class.
They did their best to keep the house clean and tidy
And washed the dishes.

Even with his new responsibilities,
Leverett continued in the seventh grade.
After school and weekends
He chopped wood, pumped water, and tended the garden.
He kept a loaded rifle on the wall beside his bed.

1912.

Papa found a stepmother for his five children.
It had taken four years.
She was a widow with a son of her own.
Eight of them lived together in the three-room house,
Attempting friendship as best they could.
There were no more babies.
The path between the front door and the porch step
Slowly abraded deeper into the raw wood.
Mattie married and moved out.
For reasons known only to her and Papa,

She took four-year-old Mary Opal with her.
Two years later Leverett enlisted in the Army.

1919.

World War I was over.
Leverett, a decorated sergeant, had survived the infantry trenches.
He transferred to the Signal Corps and remained on active duty.
Three years later Papa died
And left Mary Opal his gold watch.

At a county fair canteen,
Elva Lea met a newly discharged German-Catholic tank driver
Who had fought on the American side
Against descendants of his own ancestors.
Short and stocky,
Ed was handsome and tough.
He had a raspy deep voice and often mingled words with gusto and laughter.
Although he was not a churchgoer,
Elva Lea became a convert.
They were married in the local parish,
And she became a practicing Catholic for life.
Try as they would,
They never had children.

Pulling a small canteen trailer behind their Model T Ford,
They traveled dirt roads to rural carnivals and fairs.
Perhaps Ed did a little bootlegging on the side,
But mainly,
In heat, dust, noise, and wind,
They served eggs, burgers, and homemade pies that Elva Lea baked at dawn,
And cold bottles of Coca-Cola they plucked from tanks of ice water.

After the midway lights went dim,
They counted their money
For exchange the next day at the closest bank
Into large-denomination bills Ed kept in his wallet.

He was never robbed,
Perhaps because people knew he had served in the Army,
And carried a loaded pistol.

They worked long hours,
During and after which they smoked,
Drank black coffee,
Sometimes nursed beers hidden under the counter,
And ate the same cooking they sold.
He called her "the missus."
She loved that.
On the road,
They slept in a tent beside the canteen.
Off-season they stayed in cabin camps.
Hundreds of customers and stall mates
Were first-name acquaintances,
But they had no close friends.
They just had each other.

1928.

One slow midweek summer morning,
They rented a Chevrolet Roadster
From a gambler who needed extra money in a hurry.
Off they went on a busman's holiday to the nearby town.
The Sunflower was the restaurant where they ate.
It had starched tablecloths, real napkins, and saucers under the cups.

With the top down in the hot wind, driving back to the fair,
They fantasized about selling everything
And settling down to open a café of their own.

When they turned back into the field behind their canteen,
They saw people milling about.
Without time to change into work clothes,
Ed raised the canopies,
Elva Lea lit the grill.
Smiles and orders were quickly on the way.

1929.

More people than ever came to small-town carnivals and fairs.
If horses were racing,
Attendance was exceptionally good.
The most food of all was sold on the hottest days.
When Ed was able to buy dry ice and bulk ice cream from local suppliers,
Crowds surged the canteen so tightly
That Elva Lea stuck to frying burgers,
And he, with much stronger forearms,
To dipping vanilla, strawberry, and chocolate for hours on end.

The last week in October,
Prairie life quickly began to change.
First, money dried up,
Then the land,
Then the topsoil blew away.
Elva Lea and Ed skimped through the next six years,
Sharing subsistent communal resources
In nearly abandoned wide places along empty country roads.
As often as possible they slept in their tent.
When the weather was too cold,
Or the dust storms too intense,
They took dwindling money from Ed's wallet,
Temporarily rented a one-room shack,
And plugged the door and window cracks with newspapers.
At their eleventh hour of hope,
The WPA and rain saved them from destitution.
People began again to have money and wanted fun.
Carnivals and fairs were back on the map.

1939.

War in Europe was inexorably dragging America into its vortex,
Then the powder keg exploded at Pearl Harbor.
Ed, too old to re-enlist,
Assimilated into the home-front war effort.
During the Depression

He had learned that country and small-town junk had value.
He knew where to find it,
How to buy it,
And how to sell it:
Wood and rags to become paper,
Rusted metals to become ingots,
Old grease to become dynamite.
He also took advantage of a black-market demand for used neon signs.

Bankers soon knew his name.
He bought Elva Lea a Lincoln-Zephyr at an estate auction
And a nice corner house on West Main Street in Lorger,
Three blocks from the downtown central intersection.
She fondly called it *my shack*.
In the long backyard toward the east side street,
He built two rental bungalows.

Fifteen years after he and Elva Lea had eaten at The Sunflower,
They built Ed's Dine and Dance with a stainless-steel façade
And two large oval windows on the street.
The front half was a diner,
The back half was a combination pool hall/dance hall
That offered both diner food and cold bottled beer.
Elva Lea baked pies, cooked,
And supervised the dishwashers.
Three shifts of hired waitresses served the food.
Ed manned the cash register,
Controlled access to the back room
Through a wrought iron gate with an electromagnetic lock,
And maintained order therein.
They sold punchboard chances for a quarter,
Gum and cigarettes by the pack,
And souvenir tokens
That somehow found their way into backroom card and domino games.
Although they recommend Raleighs
Because they got a bonus strip of four gift coupons for themselves from each carton,

Ed smoked Parliaments
And Elva Lea smoked Kools.

A diamond on his little finger,
A diamond in each of her ear lobes,
And a two-carat diamond on her third finger
Were affirmations to themselves,
More than to anyone else,
Not all well-to-do small-town people
Inherit money.

1950.

Oklahoma was dry.
Two years after the Kansas Liquor Control Act became law,
They sold the Dine and Dance,
Built another building a block away,
And secured a license for the only liquor store
Between the Kansas line and the Texas border.
They worked Mondays through Saturdays
In staggered shifts all day and into the night
Until they could no longer endure the grind.

Upon their retirement,
Spike, their Boston terrier, became a constant companion.
They raised tropical fish in two 300-gallon aquariums in their living room
And in an enclosed side-porch hatchery full of repurposed Army surplus battery jars.
They grew prize roses in terraced beds,
And watched their black-and-white 21-inch console television
With a remote control—connected by a long wire
Between the set and their companion platform rockers.
They never took a vacation
And seldom traveled to the nearest city, fifty miles away.

1965.

After Ed's funeral,
Elva Lea converted her beloved shack into a duplex,

And she had her earrings and Ed's diamond mounted in a platinum dinner ring.
Sometimes in her empty bed at night,
She would roll the ring between her right thumb and middle finger,
And recall the long journey
That began in a tiny bungalow scarcely a hundred miles away,
A place where eight people tried to reconstitute a family
And failed.

A Hundred-Year Wind

In 1917 Eddie was fifteen years old.
The day his older brother, Russell, went off to war,
Their father gave them each an acorn from beneath the family's oak tree.
  "Plant these somewhere.
  If they grow, okay, if they don't, okay.
  It is the planting that is important."

Eddie chose a spot above a riverbank
Where his brother had taught him how to fish.
Russell planted his in northern France
Beside a tumbled-down cemetery wall
That shielded him through a night
He had not expected to survive.

In 1919 the war was over.
Russell was a sergeant who returned home in one piece
To marry Margaret, his sweetheart who waited,
And resume his job as a farm machinery mechanic.
Eddie worked in his father's small grocery store
And dreamed of airplanes.

The brothers went fishing, what was to be the last time,
And shared where they planted their acorns.
Russell told of France and Belgium, cold wet trenches, mustard gas, and influenza,
But not a word about the killing he himself had done,
Or of blood and guts spewed out of human beings
On both sides of the battlefield.

Eddie's greatest fascination
Was the skillful way Russell smoked an army cigarette.
He lit it in the wind by cupping balled fingers around the flame,
Then grasped the paper stick with a tent of five fingers,
Held like a cootie catcher,
As he took deep drags without revealing the pulsing glow.

Eddie was soon doing it himself.
When summer came,
With money he saved from his wages at the store,
He bought a straw boater, a double-breasted suit,
And began hawking flights for barnstorming pilots,
Who eventually taught him how to fly.

His was a gift for gab,
And he became very good at how he used it.
At twenty-one he married Patsy.
Seventeen years later their only child, Ian, was born.
Germany was conquering Europe.
Japan was soon to bomb Pearl Harbor.

Having given up flying to settle down and manage a Safeway store,
And being two years too old for the draft,
Eddie took a munitions factory job to support the war effort.
He had a security clearance,
Learned how to make bomb detonators,
And could not discuss his work.

He bought government savings bonds,
Donated blood to the Red Cross every eight weeks,
And grew vegetables, strawberries, and melons in a ten-by-ten-foot victory garden.
Everything he purchased was rationed, including four gallons of gasoline a week.
Tires were driven until they were bald.
The national speed limit was thirty-five miles per hour.

During the postwar recovery period, domestic commerce exploded.
GIs were paid to seek employment, learn a trade, or attend college.
They bought homes with no-down-payment loans.
Russell seized an opportunity to move to the northwest
And start a business of his own, maintaining apple-farm machinery.
Eddie returned to Safeway.

The greatest threat on people's minds was polio.
Then the domino effect of Communism precipitated the Korean Conflict.

In what was never officially called a war,
Ten million American men were issued draft notices,
1.8 million saw combat.
Eddie worked in the motor pool at an aircraft plant.

Three years after an armistice ended the fighting,
Escalating threats plunged into intercontinental dares approaching absolute zero.
Children, freed from the risk of catching polio,
Were drilled in school to squat, bend over, and cover their necks,
As though they could somehow survive a thermonuclear attack.
Eddie sold household appliances and turned fifty-four.

Friday, October 4, 1957, a 23-inch metallic sphere was hurled into space
To circle the earth every hour and a half.
Its beep . . . beep . . . beep
Evoked an Orwellian image of surveillance and death raining from the heavens.
Meanwhile, terrestrial conflict was developing in a jungle.
Seemingly friendly people by day became guerrilla enemies at night.

Eddie watched events unfold in black-and-white television news reports.
Ian, Eddie's son and only child, turned seventeen.
Ian was aware of escalating racial tension in the South,
But in the North,
Race was not the greatest hindrance to college admission;
It was money.

He chose a fast-track curriculum toward a degree,
And maximized part-time grocery store employment to make it possible.
In preparation for military obligation upon graduation,
He took R.O.T.C. classes with 7:00 a.m. field drills,
Opted not to enlist for an advance commission,
And was able to continue deferment into graduate school.

Thereafter, he received a direct commission as a reserve officer
And served three years on active duty in the Air Force.
The government's acquiescence to the country's outcry eventually was,

"Enough!"
And the unfortunate sacrifice of 58,000 American war-dead ended in withdrawal.
Before the last flag was lowered,
Both Russell and Eddie had died from lung cancer.

Twenty-eight years later Paul sat at his Midtown Manhattan desk on a Tuesday morning.
A few blocks away in Lower Manhattan,
His company was the largest tenant
In two of the tallest buildings in the world.
But for his low seniority,
His desk would have been there instead of where it was.

Both buildings became rubble in one hour, twenty-two minutes on live television.
In associated actions,
A portion of the Pentagon
And an airliner in a Pennsylvania field
Were gone in instants . . .
All in the name of a vengeful god.

Paul called Ian and his mother, who did not yet know.
"I'm okay, Mom and Dad, I'm okay."
Not in the aftermath,
Nor during the year before he left New York,
And not during any New York trip since,
Has Paul gone to the site where it happened.

Today younger men and women than Paul
Go forth to fight an enemy in a battle that may prove to be interminable.
His two-year-old son, Gerald, has no idea
There are boys just like him
Who have already begun indoctrination into *why*,
And soon *how*,
To eliminate infidels.

Balancing power with weapons able to annihilate the human race
Has become the insane way opposing nations avoid using them.
But what of radical suicidal martyrs and crusading zealots?

Somewhere there is a large oak tree in a copse of oaks near a riverbank.
It grew from one of two acorns Gerald's great-great-grandfather gave away,
The other, planted beside a cemetery wall 5,000 miles beyond, failed to
germinate.

Then and Now

When the American glade was painted,
It was inevitable Western Front trenches would soon include American soldiers.
The piece is signed *R J Bosence 1915*.

    Without sun or shadow,
    Or the presence of anything with a beating heart,
    It is morning beside a lake.
    Subtle ripples blur the reflection of distant snowcapped mountains.
    Nearly colorless sky silhouettes thin clouds.
    Short green and golden grasses splotch a barren clearing.
    A four-wall canvas tent on the left
    —its flaps folded away from the black interior—
        has a knapsack, a blanket, and a towel flung partway over its roof.
    In front, smoke curls from a diminishing fire beside a cast iron kettle
        suspended from a pole between two forked branches.
    A fallen tree trunk and moss-covered boulders mark the foreground.

The scene is either a refuge *from* war, or a nonmilitary alternative *to* war.
It awaits someone:

    To catch fish,
    To collect more wood,
    To whittle,
    To listen to wind in the tall trees,
    To eat, drink, and warm at the fire,
    To repose absorbed in thought, or study,
    To read, write, or make music,
    To slumber freely in safety.

More than eighty years it hung above one fireplace,
Then another,
Then I bought it at an estate sale and replaced the frame
After it became damaged in a cross-country move.

I stored the rococo discard on a spike in the shed
Above seldom used tools and a bicycle with flat tires.

From time to time a haunting glimmer from the cracked scrollwork
Beckoned me into the gaping portal from which imagination had been removed.

Eventually more room was needed in the shed,
And the frame had to go.
Rather than give it away, sell it,
Or throw it away,
A camouflage repair and a new beveled glass mirror
Brought it back into the living room.

On the opposite wall hangs the 1915 painting it once contained:
A contradiction to the grip of a war that was to end all wars,
But did not.
I can analyze its light, shade, and brushstrokes,
And reflect upon its context,
But R J Bosence is not alive to offer contemporaneous insight into how it actually was
When his paint was fresh upon the canvas.
He was the one for whom the smoldering fire waited,
In whose stead I now stand before his easel.

When I turn around and look in the mirror,
I am in the foreground of the painting in reverse.
On the wall above the mirror,
Salvaged from an antique electric metal sign,
Hang three rusted lowercase letters without punctuation:
n o w

Day and night.

Unexpected Transfer

In a dream
He tried hard.
It was not hard enough.
He had done all he could.
It still was not enough.
He was heavy-laden.
Rest would be enough.

All day he waited at the bus stop
For the right bus that did not come.
On the bench to rest beside him
Came a homeless man,
And then a homeless woman with a child.
None of them spoke
In the peaceful darkness.

Far down the road,
One pinpoint of light became two,
Then a third emerged.
It was a sliver of the destination sign.
The three homeless people rose
To form a line at the loading stanchion.
He then took up the rear.

When the bus stopped,
The spurting hiss of the locked brakes
Signaled the door was opening.
No one got off.
Although the bus was empty,
The driver called down the steps,
"There is only room for three passengers."

The three homeless people boarded.
"Please, I have waited all day for you to come.
I am tired and I need to be on this bus."
The driver, in a kind, compelling voice, replied,

"This is not the bus you need now.
Here is a transfer
That will take you back from whence you came."

Glancing down with a reassuring smile,
He closed the door
And drove away.
He who was left
Crossed the street,
And in the peaceful darkness
Awoke before the return bus arrived.

In a Glass of Confidence

His name was Wilbur.
He was a gregarious little boy with wide, lustrous blue eyes
And a continuous broad smile.
When he and Grandfather went places together,
Grandfather tousled his blond hair and introduced him to strangers saying,
"This little guy is my grandson."
Most of the time it was not followed by "Wilbur,"
So the appellation stuck.
He became known as Guy.

Her birth certificate read Constance,
But from the beginning she was Connie.

It was the roaring twenties.
The round-faced handsome young man in a boater hat with a red and blue band
And the raven-haired beauty in a periwinkle-blue cloche with appliquéd flowers
Honeymooned in his new black Good Maxwell Roadster.
They drove to Kansas City,
Made the rounds of speakeasies,
Danced the Charleston,
Drank bootlegged liquor until 2:00 a.m.,
And made love until dawn.

He was a dapper dresser with a golden charm who loved automobiles,
A born car salesman for whom, if necessary, buyers would stand in line.
Connie and Guy had met at a racetrack.
Exciting, carefree life flowed in their blood
Like the roar, wind, and dust the cars made
As they streaked by the yelling grandstand crowds.
Go, go, go!
Nothing but joy filled their lives.
Connie had been a clerk in a real estate office.
Now she was Mrs. Guy Pennington, housewife,
Providing a hot cooked breakfast every morning,

An immaculate, stylish, light-filled apartment from which to send him off,
A cozy lair with a candlelight supper ready when he returned from work.
It took her an hour to prepare it
And an hour before that to bathe, dress, brush her hair, and apply makeup.
He was her prince.
She loved being his wife *to the depth and breadth and height her soul could reach.*
Although they tried hard to have children it did not happen.

They cherished ten glorious years of wonder and opportunity
In bliss they took for granted would last forever . . .
Until it didn't.

Dust storms, drought, and near demise of the financial system
Decreased much of the nation's buying power to subsistence.
Guy lost his job and was unable to find steady reemployment.
Female telephone and comptometer operators had jobs,
But the market for high school–educated, untrained women was nonexistent;
Even department stores went through round after round of layoffs.
Connie did not grumble.
She could make a one-wiener soup last two days,
And keep their old clothes spotlessly clean in the bathroom sink.
They braved on together.

When Pearl Harbor was attacked
And war called away every young able-bodied man,
Guy was too old for induction into field combat.
Without a college education or requisite skill to be eligible for a direct commission,
He became an inspector on an aircraft assembly line.
He knew in his heart the work he was doing was essential to the war effort,
Yet day in and day out being known only as inspector B-172Q9 was stultifying.
He craved to reclaim the confidence and recognition he left in the twenties.

When the war was over and peril gave way to flourishing opportunity,
He had a chance.
Automobile sales were booming.

In spite of how many cars he sold,
How unwaveringly faithful his repeat customers were,
How many prominent buyers shook his hand
And called him by name wherever they saw him,
He could not shake the feeling that impending anonymity
Might once again be just around the corner.

After selling cars at four dealerships in nine years,
The kudos with which he most identified
He received in a tavern where he stopped on his way home from work.
Not one of these people had bought a car from him,
But when he came through the door and the shrewd bartender called out,
"Hi, Guy! One cold Schlitz comin' up,"
And the dozen or so regulars echoed the welcome,
He belonged.

Hours later, behind the wheel of a spotless, new demonstrator,
He drove home with concerted effort.
His pockets were nearly empty.
The money had gone for shuffleboard and beer.

It was often 10:30 or 11:00 at night.
Connie stayed awake to meet him,
Rewarm his supper,
Endure his ranting rebukes of her pleas for him to come home earlier,
And then submitted to his sloppy sexual needs.

Eventually he began stashing half pints of vodka
On the top shelf in the hall closet
And in a small canvas gym bag he took to work.

The Wednesday morning he was fired from his fifth job in new-car sales
For on-the-job intoxication,
And once again forfeited a demonstrator,
He did not head to the Blue Tail Fly Tavern.
He walked two miles straight home under the bright July sun.
His loosened tie, starched white shirt, and dark blue serge suit were wet with sweat.

Connie was hanging bed sheets and towels on the clothesline
And did not hear him enter the house.
She found him sitting in front of the living room fan in his briefs and undershirt,
With a bottle of Schlitz in his hand.

"Hi."
She knew at once what had happened again.
"I put my clothes in the hamper."
"Your suit too?"
"Yes, my suit too!"
"Oh, Guy!"
"Don't you start in on me too! I've had a rough morning."

He went to bed and slept fifteen hours.
Next day he arose as usual,
Halfheartedly told her he was sorry for yelling at her,
Took a bath, put on a sport shirt and wash pants,
And caught the bus downtown to apply for unemployment compensation.

The clerk helped him hire back into the aircraft factory.
Once again he carried a dinner bucket, rode in a carpool
... and hated it.
He smuggled vodka into the plant by lacing the coffee in his thermos.
Because he did not have a car,
After-work tavern stops were out of the question.

In a month he quit,
Listing incompatible foot and varicose vein problems as the reason.
He resumed applying for jobs
And was required to report to the unemployment office once a week.
A cocky attitude worked wonders to foil the interviews they arranged for him.
The rest of his time he spent at Pace's Bait Shop and Tavern.
It was as far away from the Blue Tail Fly as he could get.

On the second-to-last day before the unemployment benefit checks were to cease,
He took a job selling used cars for a dealer who bought at secondary market auctions.

Nobody knew where the cars came from or anything about their true conditions.
The pay was 100 percent commission, and the owner set a high weekly quota
That drove his salesmen into cutthroat competition.
At the back of the lot were three junk trade-ins they could drive home at night.
It was inconsequential that the clunkers were not close to a demonstrator's status,
Because at 10:00 p.m.,
After working thirteen hours,
And sneaking nips of vodka throughout the day,
Guy was exhausted and went straight home to sleep.

After seven humiliating weeks of not making his quota,
When the other two salesmen were making theirs
And were eager to pick up the few sales he was taking away from them,
Once again he found himself out of a job.

Spiraling downward and striking out at two more used-car lots,
There were no more dealers to approach.

The day before he and Connie were to be evicted,
They signed over the equity in their home to a neighbor
In exchange for moving expenses
And money to cover a month's rent in a tiny apartment.

One week later,
A morning he left early on the premise of looking for a job,
Connie tied one wrist to the bathtub faucet
And with a double-edge razor blade
Slit both wrists and drank a cup of lye.

She had married him when she was twenty-one
And had been faithful thirty-two years.
She had been his anchor to the end of lifting her pen
From the last "*e*" of "*Connie*" on her suicide note.
It told him she was sorry to do this at the time of his greatest need.
She could not help him anymore because she could not go on herself.
She had run out of hope.

To pay for her funeral he took out an installment loan on their furniture.
Upon missing the first payment it was repossessed.
A week thereafter, the electricity, gas, and telephone services were turned off.
He returned in the dark to sleep in the empty apartment,
But something was wrong.
Why did the key not work?
He sat down to think about it and promptly fell asleep against the door jamb.

Someone was shaking him,
It was morning.
The policeman led him to a patrol car and ducked him into the backseat.
Never in his life had he been in trouble with the law.
Now he was standing before a desk sergeant trying to explain himself.

"See, here is my key."
"The reason it did not work is that the landlord changed the lock.
Do you have any family who can come and get you?"
"No."

"The landlord is not pressing charges.
So, it won't do you or us any good to book you for vagrancy.
Officer Simpson, take him to the Inner City Mission."

Guy was dumbfounded.
Back in the patrol car he stared into oblivion through the side window.
The policeman had to pull him out and lead him into the converted old church.

"Gert, here's another one.
He was found sleeping on a doorstep where he used to live.
No trouble, no record.
See ya next time."

Stripped of all dignity,
Guy just stood there, vaguely aware of someone behind a reception counter.

"Are ya hungry?"
He had to think.
"No."

"What's yur name?"
"Guy."
"Cum'in, Guy. Beds r'in the back.
Doors open between 11:30 and 1:00 for soup and a sandwich.
Doors open again at 5:30.
Ya need to be at a table by 6:00 when singing and bible study starts.
After that ya'cun eat and take a shower.
We only have four, so ya hav'ta wait yur turn.
Lights out at 9:30. Up at 6:30.
Breakfast at 7:00 and yur outta here no later than 8:00.
Ya can come for soup and a sandwich as long as ya want,
But ya can only sleep here three nights in a row.
Any questions?"
"No."

He did not return for lunch.
He spent the afternoon in Box Park.
It came to him:

> *What about my brother Fred?*
> *I have not seen him for at least twenty-five years.*
> *Is he still alive?*
> *If so, where is he?*

That night at the mission he lay awake planning what to do.
He would go to the library first thing in the morning.
He was there when it opened at ten o'clock.
Researching the first question took all day.
Fred had been in World War I.
The librarian showed Guy how to access the microfiche military records.
Unless he had died within the past two years,
There was no record of a veteran's death benefit being paid.
He remembered Fred was selling real estate the last time he saw him.
Next day, back again when the library opened,
A research intern found Fred was listed fifteen years previously
In a National Association of Real Estate Boards directory.
The place was California.

Searching a series of city directories, then a current telephone directory,
Revealed a listing for Fred in San Jose.
Guy told the intern he had no money.
He offered her his watch for the chance to make a phone call.
She was not about to take the watch,
But neither was she authorized to allow him to call long distance.
Presenting the dilemma to her supervisor,
The woman carried it up the chain of command high enough
For approval of a five-minute station-to-station call.
It was successful.

Fred and his wife Julia bought Guy a bus ticket to San Jose.
On the condition he would not drink in the presence of their guests,
They let him sleep on a rollaway bed in the storeroom of a motel they managed.
They bought him a suit and helped him get a job selling Ramblers.
Once again, he had a brand new demonstrator, gasoline, and car washes.
Soon he was able to move to a rooming house that offered meals.

He told Mrs. B he would eat her breakfasts,
But he worked late, and the Bridge Café and Tavern were on his way home,
So he would eat there before coming in at night.

He bought a briefcase in which he carried sales brochures,
NADA and Blue Books, financing and order forms,
And a half-pint flask in a snappable pocket.

He resurrected his old drinking routine,
And the charade failed again.
He lost his job.
His brother would not take him back.

Somehow he was able to enroll for public assistance and a flophouse bed.

After years of constantly using gum, mints, and Sen-Sen
To mask halitosis and the telltale smell of alcohol,
The sugar had rotted his teeth.
The smile that all his life had ingratiated him to people was gone.

When he could no longer endure the pain,
He went to the county hospital for extraction of the snaggletooth stumps.
Five days later when he returned to have the stitches taken out,
The dentist struck up a conversation.
Much more than that,
He listened.

Guy began to tell him about automobile inventions he had experienced:
Electric starters, heaters, radios, automatic drives, power brakes, and power steering.
With encouragement he began to remember more.
The dentist had tapped into an old spark in the once purposeful salesman
Who took pride in his integrity.
His goal had been to sell automobiles that were right for his customers
—not the most expensive models he could push them into—
Models that looked good, performed well, and were what they could afford.

The dentist began to reflect on his own transcendent purpose.
He had taken care of Guy's pain and suffering,
And could let him walk out the door
Having fulfilled his Hippocratic obligation.
Instead, he asked Guy for a commitment.

"If you will show up for every appointment and not imbibe a drop of alcohol
During the four days it will take to do it,
I will make you a complimentary set of dentures."

Guy had not been able to get through four days without alcohol for a long time.
With tears in his eyes,
He told the dentist something he had never accepted or admitted to anyone:
"I am an alcoholic.
I would like to have new teeth more than anything,
But I can't live without a drink
. . . I can't live without a drink."

"But you can try,
That's all I ask.
How about this,
What if I see you first thing every day,
And we take the four days one at a time?
You know what?
You can already chalk up the first day,
And you have already admitted to yourself
You have a problem over which you have no control."

Somehow drawing the courage to do so,
Guy earned the teeth.
They were not free.
He had paid a very high price.

The fourth and last day,
When the dentist inserted the new dentures
And handed Guy a mirror to take a look,
The smile Guy saw had traveled through infinity to get there.

"Guy,
It is entirely up to you to take care of that smile.
I'm not just talking about conscientious scrubbing and Polident soaks every day
—don't get me wrong, they're essential too—
I'm talking about what is inside of you that lets that smile happen.
Here is a card with the name of a man who can help you help yourself.
He can be your new brother in a family you can cherish
. . . and they can be your family the rest of your life."

Guy lived eleven years after that.
He developed a talent he had ignored since childhood
And became a successful pen-and-ink artist
Whose political cartoons in newspapers found their way into millions of homes
Twice a week.
His signature in the lower right corner of each drawing
Was accompanied by a hallmark:

A small hand mirror,
On the glass of which were two words,
Almost indecipherable because they were so small:
. . . *Dear Connie.*

Parental Guidance

Brian Candle Jerry was a magnolia tree
Two six-year-old boys appropriated for the crow's nest of a brig
In which they ventured on waves of wind above the housetops
To imaginary places inhabited by great swashbucklers.

Four years later, in a backyard hundreds of miles away,
The large oak tree with lowest branches well above the reach of a six-foot ladder
Held no imagination for the ten-year-old former seafarer
Whose sister was now the age he was when *Brian Candle Jerry* was as real as a ship.

She found magic in the rundown detached garage
On a platform above the hood of the family car parked beneath.
Climbing the shelves of a tool cabinet along the wall to get there,
She named the space *Downstairs*.

Her brother liked it so well
—and because fifth grade entitled him to an advantage over first grade—
He created *Upstairs* in the rafters above it all
On a sheet of plywood put there years before to store scrap pipes and lumber.

Their parents,
Conflicted between hazard and overprotection,
Counseled them on the risk of falling
And entrusted them with the privacy of a precarious clubhouse.

A neighbor who saved everything
Gave them four worn-out tires they covered with blankets.
Their mother contributed throw pillows for the centers,
And—voilà!—they had lounge chairs.

A girl the same age as the boy
Lived in a house on the street behind the garage.
One day she was sharing Barbie dolls with his sister *Downstairs*,
The next, day she was helping him write *Upstairs* club rules.

Both *Upstairs* and *Downstairs* had cigar boxes for treasures.
He had a battery-operated transistor radio, made balsa wood models,
And created a board game about buried treasure.
His sister made crayon drawings and played with a tea set.

Even when their mother brought iced lemonade and cookies,
An hour or two a day,
Particularly in July and August,
Was all the heat they could endure in the still, dim space.

Autumn, with shorter days, soccer games, longer bike rides,
And homework before watching television
Reduced the time they spent in what had come to be known as
Dimensional Hideout in the Garage.

Winter and spring passed.
With new friends and more distractions
—or perhaps taking for granted it would always be there—
Dimensional Hideout in the Garage was ignored and eventually returned to storage.

Decades later, sorting through a box of donated children's clothing,
The Goodwill store volunteer discarded without a thought
Two nearly threadbare white T-shirts
With faded, blue *D H G* lettering.

On two desks, a thousand miles apart,
Remnants from the cigar box have fared better.
Small stones painted white with the letters D H G painted in blue
Serve as talisman paperweights atop sheets of corporate priorities.

The Commanding General's Daughter

Behind the clearly delineated tarmac
An enlisted man watched the boarding passengers
Like cogs of gears meshing in motion.

A queer function, this military machine,
That lubricates sand in an hourglass
To move people who do not want to go.

She looked back momentarily
Around the stars on her father's shoulder,
But knowing the repercussion, did not wave.

When the stairs were rolled away,
And the engines began to whirr,
Not a single window revealed a face.

Bucking the odds was a risky venture.
He had secretly spent the night with her,
Yet was barred from asking for a legitimate date.

Not all military casualties are blood and guts,
Or posttraumatic demons of the mind.
Some can be words.

Arrogance

After traveling 93 million miles,
It would have taken one ten-thousandth of a second more
For sunlight to cross the forested valley
And reach the interstate highway beyond.
As it was,
A polka-dot array of clouds and striated sheets of rain got in the way.

This did not alter the behavior of two vehicles
Chasing one another along the mountain pass
For lead position through the storm.
Eighty miles an hour was perceived to be acceptable
Because the tires on which they rolled
Had patented antihydroplaning treads.

Looking with the Sun

From the bluff,
Dawn arises behind me
Into steel-blue sky in the west,
Over calm ocean north to south,
As shimmering corrugations roll in.

Descending to the brink,
I stoop and reach out open hands.
The water flows across my palms.
It is cool
And cleanses the new day.

Hands-On Time

Navy Seaman George Wilford
Maintained jet engines and machinery
For pilots who depended upon his care and skill
To do their jobs and return safely
From Viet Nam sorties
Flown off the aircraft carrier *Midway*.

Docking at Yokosuka,
360 degrees of deck
Was no longer a hazard,
And thirteen hundred hours
Became one o'clock in the afternoon
The first time in two years.

Separation orders in hand,
A duffle bag on his back,
His feet on the gangplank the last time,
George was on his way home
To take up where he had left off,
A mechanic at Gibson's Pontiac Agency.

He wound the wristwatch
His parents had given him at high school graduation.
The next seventy-two hours
He had looked forward to since boot camp.
Now he wondered,
Maybe he should have reenlisted?

A sailor Tuesday in Japan,
A civilian Saturday in Oakland, California,
He and his discharged buddies
Closed out the day in a bar while embellishing war stories,
Watching a World Series game,
And making reunion plans they would never keep.

Twenty-four hours later
—the first night he slept in his own bed again—

Arab nations embargoed oil,
And soon motorists waited in long lines
To put ten gallons of gasoline in twenty-two-gallon gas tanks.
Car sales slumped and repair work greatly increased.

The shop phone rang several times
Before George could scramble his creeper from under the car's chassis.
"DAMN!"
His watch crystal shattered against the tool cabinet.
"HELLO?"
Someone else had picked up the call.

Bulova advertised an Accutron,
The first mass-produced watch
Powered by a battery and a transistor.
It never needed winding,
And as its name implied,
It kept good time.

George accepted Mr. Duval's magnifying loupe
And saw how the Accutron worked:
A sliver of metal between two miniature solenoids
Vibrated so fast it appeared not to move at all,
It just hummed.
It was guaranteed to be accurate within two seconds a day.

Compared to a Navy machine shop
And Gibson's Pontiac Agency,
The tedium of one-eyed work
Mincing grain-size things inside thimbles
Interested him far less
Than the palm-size clockworks he saw on a side bench.

Mr. Duval noticed and began telling a story.
His first apprentice project,
In France before World War II,
Was to make a set of clockmaker's tools
And a small wooden box to hold them.
It took three weeks.

The story soon turned to pendulums and escapements,
Weights, springs, balance wheels, and chimes . . .
How to equate twenty-four hours of time
With one lifting of a weight,
Or one winding of a spring.
How to optimize a gear train.

George left that day with a new Accutron on his wrist
And an old pendulum clock in a bag.
During the next few months,
While they tinkered one night a week,
Mr. Duval taught him how to clean and adjust many clockworks.
In September George began horology school in Chicago.

A wife, children, a business of his own,
Thirty-six years later George received a package from Mr. Duval's widow.
It was the small wooden box of handmade tools.
Reflecting back, he removed the Accutron watch he still wore,
And placed it and Mr. Duval's tools in a glass case beside his cash register
With a sign that read *Not for Sale*.

Digital numerals on screens had been rapidly replacing analog dials.
Repair of old clocks, not the sale of new ones, kept George in business.
In space he shared with a used bookseller,
He accumulated lots of clocks;
Some he purchased, some he received as gifts,
Most were unclaimed repairs.

Location, location, location being a key factor,
Customers patronized where a business was located as much as for what it offered.
Thus, a businesswoman approached George's landlord
With a long-term lease proposal.
She was willing to pay twice the present rent
For a divided half of the current space.

The used book dealer folded rather than agree to double rent for half the space.

George had no recourse but to move.
Fifteen years he had never been late with a rent check,
Now, he had thirty days to vacate.
Not ready to retire at sixty-one years of age,
He had to scramble.

In desperation he proposed a deal to the landlord:
Partition the front space down the middle for two new tenants,
Include one of the existing two restrooms as a unisex facility on each side,
And close off the storeroom in the back that opened on the alley.
If building code regulations permitted,
He would like to rent that space as it was, even without a restroom.

The resourceful landlord accepted.
George relocated.
Two steps below ground level,
Barred windows flanked both sides of the door.
New fluorescent tubes in the old suspended ceiling fixtures
Provided adequate light.

Numeral faces were everywhere:
    Banjo, cuckoo, calendar, and school clocks on the walls,
    Mantle, statue, carriage, steeple, and porcelain clocks
    On tables, shelves, and in cabinets,
    Grandfather and street clocks on the floor,
    A large tower-face dial without works in the corner.

Like castaways in a forgotten museum vault,
Every clock's provenance had been lost.
Only their identities survived.
The remnant covenants for tens of thousands of windings
Were the clock makers' signatures
Engraved on the frames.

Ivan discovered the shop by chance.
While in one of the street-side stores,
He overheard someone ask the clerk,
"What happened to the clock repair shop that used to be somewhere around here?"

"Oh, it still is, but it is not on the street anymore.
It is in the alley."

On a future trip downtown,
Ivan brought along a cuckoo clock
His dad had inherited from an aunt many years previously.
The clock did not work,
But his dad's childhood memory of when it had
Was the reason Ivan had kept it in a box on the top shelf of his closet.

George was on the telephone when Ivan entered.
"I'm open twelve thirty until five
Most Tuesdays through Saturdays . . .
It's best to call ahead before you come . . .
I'm the only shop in the alley,
You can't miss me."

Ivan learned his clock was more than a hundred years old.
It was a Bavarian Black Forest Quail Cuckoo
Like one George pointed out on his far wall.
He wanted eight hundred dollars for it,
But he was willing to negotiate an offer
That would include Ivan's clock as a trade-in.

Ivan declined.
Instead, he had George clean and adjust the nonworking relic,
Fabricate new goatskin bellows,
Add links to one of the three chains,
Align the hammer and gong,
And calibrate the pendulum bob.

Ivan retrieved the repaired timepiece in a week.
As he exited beneath the *Tick Tock Doc of State Street Alley* sign,
He shared the doorway with a man coming in.
The man clutched a box of disassembled parts
And a cast-iron clock case.
It appeared to be a garage-sale purchase.
As the man and George laid out things on the counter,

George said to him,
"There aren't many of us left who fix old clocks.
You are wise to get it done now."
It was a statement of pride in his craftsmanship
As much as it was salesmanship of his service.

Neither Ivan nor the man realized the depth of George's implication.
The expression of time,
Like the temperature of fire or the color of light,
Is a continuum of mysterious energy,
Arbitrarily measured in mortal increments
With devices tended by adherent guardians.

Since Ctesibius in Alexandria, Greece,
More than twenty-two hundred years ago,
The skills of mechanical clock making
Have evolved through countless timesmiths
Perfecting the adjustment
Of micro moments of silence between activated ticks.

Today scientists have atomic clocks with no moving parts.
The intervals of silence between resonating pings are so precise
A strontium clock is believed neither to lose nor gain a single second
In five billion years
—approximately five hundred million years longer than the earth has existed—
How they determine this, I don't know.

Apparently modern civilization needs this precision.
Consider the television correspondent who asks a question from California
And must awkwardly await the turnaround response from Australia.
Einstein found the explanation in his inscrutable theory of relativity.
It is impossible to know a specific moment everywhere from anywhere,
When *now* is only *now* in one place at a time.

Like Ctesibius,
We live in ignorance of an exponential future.
Assuming we survive and travel vast distances with need for linkage home,

Will there eventually be a timepiece for recording omnipresent *now* the instant it *is*,
Or will *now* remain a lapse of immutable something
Between concurrent realities?

For today's moments,
The clock George restored for Ivan hangs on a wall beside a staircase.
It cuckoos every fifteen minutes throughout the house,
A subliminal reminder
That *now* is a wonderment
Not to be lost or taken for granted.

The clock runs less than a minute fast each day,
Exceeding the strontium device's error 1.825 trillion times.
Using an iPhone for reference and his index finger to interrupt the pendulum,
Ivan recalibrates the escapement once or twice a week.
In deference to George,
This is adequate.

Last Reunion

Its doors first opened seven years before they arrived as sophomores,
A broad-spectrum socioeconomic group of kids,
Who, outside the school, went their separate ways.
Here, they moved among each other,
Having but one thing they could call their own:
A hall locker.

Classrooms and the library nourished their intellects.
Athletic facilities provided physical and competitive challenges.
Studios and performance facilities tapped their creative expression.
Thirty years before text messaging would be possible,
It was during the hundred thousand footsteps seven minutes every hour
That most communication and community happened.

At 8:00 a.m. on the fiftieth autumn Saturday,
Those alive who cared to return
Gathered at the front steps.
Their words and breath-fog anticipation
Mixed with the skittering leaves
Into a crescendo of pervasive excitement.

Twenty minutes late,
A stocky man in jeans and a T-shirt,
With a photo ID and whistle lanyard around his neck,
Pushed two spring-loaded horizontal bars,
And with the never-to-be-forgotten *ka-chunk, ka-chunk* sound,
The doors opened and the crowd funneled in.

As he switched on banks of fluorescent lights,
The terrazzo-floored lobby, long central hall, and transept wings gleamed.
A large hanging red and white banner proclaimed,
Making History One Senior at a Time.
Hundreds of high-gloss goldenrod-yellow enamel lockers
Lined both sides of the corridors into their intersections with other halls.

Starting to raise his whistle to quell the noise,
Then having a second thought,

He began to speak in a loud voice.
"I am Athletic Director Pelster, assistant principal here at South Central."
Stocky, late thirties to early forties, with a swagger,
He presented himself as one to be reckoned with.

Every college and university in the country
Fronts its elite administrators for alumni events
Because alumni money is crucial to the thriving existence of those institutions.
Since South Central operated on an appropriated budget,
Athletic Director Pelster drew this assignment from a principal
Who preferred to do something other than confront alumni on a Saturday morning.

He began by touting his ascendency to athletic director/vice principal
Then segued into the school's upcoming closure in four months.
"The current epicenter of 2,000 students
Will be exchanged for a new facility six miles away
To which the current 2,000 students will go in cars
Or be transported by a fleet of busses."

Voters had approved municipal bonds six years earlier for an *additional* high school
Never imagining it would replace this, the second-largest high school in town.
Two years later, a newly elected ultraright governor slashed education funding,
Leaving the school board with just enough money to operate existing facilities.
Instead of deferring issuance of bonds for the new high school,
The board voted to transfer South Central operations from one place to another.

"What will happen to the old building once it is vacated?"
A.D.V.P. Pelster said it would be repurposed into something yet to be determined.
Until then, it might be used for school-board offices and miscellaneous storage.

Perhaps something similar was said in 1956—the year South Central was built—
When the premier Packard Motor Car Company plant in Detroit, Michigan,
Became, and remains to this day, the largest abandoned factory in the world.

As the alumni spread out,
Walked the empty halls, located old lockers,
And remembered teachers, athletic events, cafeteria food, and proms,
They trod where it actually happened,
When no one thought about remembering it
Or losing forever the opportunity to see it again.

Upward Mobility

Double-career suburbanites plunk money
Into quick deals on fast cars
So they can jump away from stoplights
And weave through traffic
Like professional drivers who drive on closed courses
In television commercials
Above small-print *Do Not Attempt* disclaimers
Everybody knows are legal absolutions
Not intended for a moment to fetter desire.

No wonder a four-lane concrete link to the freeway
Is nearly insufficient for aggressive and often cursing drivers
To cover the same five miles
Two lanes handled ten years ago,
When homogeneous houses with double garages
Began spreading over fifty-foot slices of land
As quickly as they were platted,
And *For Sale* signs lured buyers to the horizon
With claims of quick commutes to and from the city.

The only drivers who travel slowly
And journey with leisure,
Like the people here before the subdivisions,
Who traveled over a dirt road across open range
To a ranch beyond the second hill,
Are young lads in nearby backyards
Who push toy cars and trucks,
And make humming and beeping sounds for engines and horns,
Without concern for makes, models, or years.

Career Move

Two of them and their dog
Crush through leaves under a nearly bare tree beside the sandy footpath.
A bird squawks away to a nearby bush.
Thanks to the nine o'clock sun,
The cold air no longer shows their breath.
As the dog sniffs plant to plant,
Frequently pausing to lift its leg
Or raises its head toward the next guiding scent,
Her husband reaches to hold her hand.

After a while he speaks:
"We are fortunate to have moved here three years ago."
"I know."
Nothing else is said.
Walking on until the dog abruptly pulls him toward the underbrush,
He releases her hand.
Overhead to his left in the east,
A white contrail spinning from a silver aircraft dot
Drifts backward in a long, dilating ribbon.

Their granddaughter,
The little girl who plays with Cheerios in her fingers,
Who is unable to see over the stroller she enjoys pushing as much as riding,
Who loves to shake her head and hips and dance to fast music,
Who points out the moon day and night,
Who wears hats with a flair,
Is beginning to say understandable words.
Now they learn her parents are moving away,
And she will become an image on a computer screen talking to a camera.

Four years before her mother was born,
They married and moved two thousand miles from home.
Initially it was for graduate school.
Later, it was in pursuit of increasingly better job opportunities.
They never moved back.

There were letters, phone calls, and once or twice yearly visits
In which their parents most often came to see them.
Bittersweet time was always too short.
Leave-taking was painfully difficult.

First, their fathers died,
Then their mothers.
Abruptly, their children were in high school,
College, graduate school, the workforce, and married.
Parents' weekends, holidays, and shared vacations
Blended as they happened
Into negotiated plans for the next year,
When *for sure* there would be more time.
There never was until now.

The sandy path ends.
She takes his hand.
They turn left onto the sidewalk.
"The contrail is gone," he says.
"Yes," she replies.
Their dog leads the way
Behind a corrugated steel guardrail
Separating them from speeding employees
Who will not be late for work.

Life

It is my birthday.
On the patio
At the Cathedral of St. Francis in Santa Fe,
I lower my head,
Namaste,
And enter the labyrinth:
Straight, turn, travel,
Reverse,
Reverse again.
As I become more aware of the moment,
I begin to forget the journey
Behind and ahead.
I pass others and others pass me.
It starts to sprinkle.
The granite path becomes slippery.
I slow my pace.
The scattered drops turn into a shower.
I step across puddles
Until they coalesce
Into a shallow pond,
And I am getting quite wet.
I note my location
And seek shelter beneath the boundary foliage.
There is no lightning,
Only a gentle breeze
And the cleansing sound of rain.
When it stops,
I return,
But cannot find where I left off.
So, I start anew.
Namaste.
As I walk,
I pass others,
And others pass me.
It is my birthday.

Tell the Stories Now

How dear it is to remember my father to you,
As he never did for me.
The timespan is abstract,
And a little difficult to conceptualize,
But let us try to stand in the interim from my father's birth until now,
And from now until you will be the age I am today.

July 21, 2049
Will be a leap year Tuesday with a waxing moon.
My first grandchild will be thirty-eight years old.
Perhaps that day you will send her a message:

> Your grandfather was born Sunday, July 21, 1940.
> Were he alive—he died in 20xx—
> He would be 109 years old.

Obviously, that day you will not receive a message
Like I have sent you once a year since you were a child;
So I am telling you now what it would say:

> *Your grandfather was born Tuesday, October 21, 1902*
> *Were he alive—he died in 1969—*
> *He would be 147 years old in three months.*

That sounds like a long, long time
But considered another way,
It is not.
I am 75 now,
You will be 75 then.
You will be looking back to the birth of your grandfather
The way I look back to the birth of my grandfather today.
Granddad was born the year the Civil War ended,
Three years before the Great Chicago Fire,
Thirty-eight years before the Great San Francisco Earthquake,
And forty-four years before the *RMS Titanic* sank.

My father knew of this
And a lot more he never told me
Because I did not ask.

I let it slip away.

Eminent Domain

Postwar prosperity was returning on a relative scale for everyone.
People drove the best automobiles they could afford,
Even if they lived modestly at the edge of town.

In one of the two middle blocks in a four-block stretch
There were assorted houses on one side of the street
And on the other a farm, taken by the county for unpaid taxes,
Then planted with pine and elm trees and sowed with fescue.
The wide-open space was called Connection Road Park.

When it,
His own half acre,
And a mile beyond
Were annexed into the city,
Fowler subdivided off his side yard
And put both properties on the market.

The empty lot was forty-seven feet wide,
Three feet too narrow to qualify for a driveway of its own.
When the city paved the road,
A double-wide slab was poured across the property line.
The north half was aligned with the dirt driveway of the old house.
The south half was a single off-street parking space.
Workmen stamped *Eby Construction Co. 1950* into the wet cement
And moved on to the next house.
Andrew followed close behind with a large nail,
And scratched *I am Andrew* below the embossed *1950*.

His father, mother, and he
Traveled back and forth to the empty lot from their city apartment
To tend a garden and harvest more vegetables than they could eat, can, or give away.
When it didn't rain,
They carried water in a bucket
From Slansky's hand-pumped well next door.

Andrew's parents met Louis Welborn while he was building a garage
Across the alley from their apartment.
He sat at their kitchen table
And used the stub of a carpenter's pencil he sharpened with a pocketknife
To sketch a one-story, 32-feet-by-32-feet bungalow.
A subsequent blueprint of the plan was granted a city building permit
And approved for a $6,000 FHA loan.

Throughout fall and winter
Louis and Eldon,
The whiskered old guy in a smashed felt hat he never removed,
And the strapping lad, who followed directions and never said a word,
Did the carpentry and subcontracted out the remainder.
The address was 1736.

At the north end of the block,
Newlyweds Nadine and Bill Poor were 1702.
Theirs was a flat-roof, pale-yellow stucco house.
Bill was a stockman for Western Auto Supply.
He drove a new black Ford convertible
Modified with dual glasspack mufflers,
Rear fender skirts,
And blue-dot taillights that at a distance glowed like purple fuzz in the night.
Nadine was a cafeteria cashier.

1708 was Howard and Doris Strella's house.
Except for being pastel aqua,
It was identical to the Poors.
The Strellas had a maroon two-door Studebaker
With a bullet grille and panoramic rear window.
Howard worked at a feed-and-poultry store.
Doris was a homemaker with young twins.
Kit and Britt were *The Neighborhood Handful.*

At 1712 lived the Maxwells.
Rod was a self-employed plumber
Who drove an International Harvester panel truck,
Into which he, Wilma, Donna, and Harold

Crowded four abreast when they went places as a family.
They lived in a converted boxcar covered with aluminum-painted tar paper.
Wilma took in laundry she washed in a wringer machine
And dried on clotheslines longer than the house.
Her ironing was flawless.
Donna wore bobbysocks and white saddle oxfords.
She carried books eight blocks back and forth to school
In her arms crossed over her chest.
Harold had curly hair.
He clamped playing cards on his bicycle fenders with clothespins.
The clicks against the spokes resembled a motorcycle.

Sam and Evelyn Yarbrough were grandparents who lived at 1718
In a white cement-block house with a pitched metal roof.
Sam drove a gray-green Nash shaped like an upside-down bathtub with a sun visor.
He was an upholsterer for a restaurant supply company,
Evelyn was a homemaker.
They raised Irish Setters and used Connection Park to train them to point.
The mailman bought one to accompany him on his rounds.

1722.
The Litseys—Everett, Maud, and their sons Clinton and Lloyd—
Lived in a white frame house with a porch clear across the front.
Their blue and white Buick had fake exhaust ports on the front fenders.
Everett was a tool-and-die maker for the railroad,
Maud was a homemaker.
Clinton threw morning papers at 5:30 and evening papers after school.
He did homework and practiced on a portable Smith Corona typewriter
By fluorescent light at a small desk in the front window.
He saved his paper-route money to go to college.
Instead,
The summer after high school,
He married and went to work in his father-in-law's alignment and brake shop.

1724 was Earl and Ruth Henderson and their two daughters.
Betty, the younger,

Caught polio and was quarantined a full summer.
Large black letters on a yellow sign fastened beside the front door
Cautioned people to stay away.
When she returned to school soon after Thanksgiving,
She walked with a sway and slightly drug her left leg.
Her parents drove a brown Mercury.
Her mother, Ruth, took in sewing.
Earl was a sheet metal worker at a floor-furnace company.

Bob and Louise Slansky were young Catholics who lived next door at 1732.
They had four children: Dick, Ralph, Roberta, and Butch.
The rundown house they bought from Fowler was similar to the Litseys,
Except it had two front doors at opposite ends of the front porch.
Louise worked part-time at St. James Hospital.
Bob rebuilt Caterpillar bulldozer engines.
A large man who drank too much,
He and Louise often fought loud arguments with their windows open.
Sometimes he punched her, for which she made vague, weak excuses.
One evening, alone on his way home from work with an open bottle in the glove box,
He fell asleep at the wheel and was thrown out when his Oldsmobile turned over.
He died instantly of a broken neck.

The open casket was covered with a gauze shroud.
The Catholic church was so full,
Many people sat on folding chairs in the parish hall.
Bob's parents were tightfisted farmers with oil wells on their land.
They had given Bob and Louise the Oldsmobile as a wedding present
—but nothing else.
After Bob's death,
His life insurance and their remorse
Provided money for Louise to buy a new Pontiac, quit work, and fix up her house.
She did not remarry.

1736 was Andrew's house.
It was a bungalow with wide clapboard siding.

His father, James, was a wholesale grocery salesman who worked on commission
And did not take vacations.
He drove a company car.
Andrew's mother, Patsy, wore a hearing aid.
Weekdays she provided daycare for working mothers.
The outside doors were not left open unless the screen doors were hooked
Because the street was unchecked by a stop sign half a mile in either direction.
When a driver killed Andrew's dog, Skippy,
Beneath wheels that left no evidence of a skid mark,
Andrew and his dad set iron posts and stretched a wire fence around the backyard.
They adopted another dog, Poncho,
And in nice weather the daycare children could play outside.
To keep the grass green without having an enormous water bill,
They drilled a well.
The quarter-horse electric motor and Army surplus pump
Delivered enough water for two hoses.
Andrew cut the resulting grass with a push mower
And emptied the catcher in the alley behind the fence.
Every few weeks, on a day when wind was not blowing, he burned the dry clippings.

Wind was often a factor in work done outside.
It certainly was after a harsh winter's toll on the north side of the house.
They spread thick white paint evenly back and forth,
Working it into the wood without leaving streaks.
It was noontime when they reached the lower level of the windowsills.
They broke for lunch and his dad listened to the noon news on the radio.
By the time they got back outside, the wind had come up.
Every square inch of fresh paint was heavily flocked with cottonwood seeds
From Slansky's backyard tree.
It took a full day to sand off the damage.

Another day, wind was blowing when they moved the television antenna
From the attic to a rooftop pole for better reception of a CBS station fifty miles away.

Andrew's mother chided them, "Come down, you'll break your necks!"
Although they too were concerned,
They proceeded with affected bravado until the job was finished.
The test pattern looked good,
But when the station signed on that afternoon,
Snow on the screen was the same as before.

Next door south at 1742 was where the Goodies lived.
Their converted boxcar home was similar to the Maxwells,
Except it had white asbestos shingle siding in place of aluminum painted tar paper.
On warm Friday nights,
They moved their living room furniture into the back of Clemet's dump truck,
Took it to the double feature at the Meadowlark Drive-in Theater,
Then brought it home at midnight and carried it back inside.
No one ever accepted an invitation to go with them.
One day they loaded up everything they had and left an hour or two
Before the sheriff came to evict them.

Buddy and Fern Pratt bought the repossession at a bank auction.
They filled in the privy and added an indoor bathroom.
Buddy had lived in an orphanage until he was adopted at nine years of age.
He was a jovial guy who delivered bread for Rainbow Bakery.
Fern was a homemaker.
Their car was a gray Ford with back doors that opened toward the front.
Summer afternoons the sound of Fern playing ragtime music on her upright piano
Mingled with the whirr of an evaporative cooler sucking air through wet excelsior.
Andrew knew how she kept such a good tan.
It was by lying in the backyard sun on a chaise lounge
In very short shorts and a very skimpy halter she untied when she turned face down.
After she and Buddy adopted Steven and had little time to play ragtime music,
Andrew no longer had incentive to mow grass during the hottest part of the day.

Dale and JoAnn Grunder lived in a bungalow at 1748.
It had a high foundation four steps above the ground.
They drove a green Frazer with wide white sidewall tires.
Dale had been a soldier in the South Pacific,
And was active in the VFW.
Monday through Friday at 6:00 a.m. on the dot
A carpool honked to take him to his job as a lineman for the electric company.
JoAnn was a homemaker.
She paid no attention to the neighbors,
But frequently came and went places with her young daughter.
She had lots of company.
It was rumored the women came to buy housewares and cosmetics.

1750 was the only house on the block with either an attached garage or a basement.
It had both.
Leo Grey was shop foreman at Churchill Chevrolet,
Marie was a homemaker.
They got a new Chevy every year.
Their son Jerry was a good softball player.
When the boys chose off teams,
Eddie Hardison from the 1600 block was selected first
Because he was the best slugger.
Jerry was second.
With his trapper's mitt,
He could reach higher and scoop the ground better than anyone else.
On rainy days he invited friends to play with the electric train in his basement.

1752 was at the south end of the block.
It had a two-story unfinished addition at the back.
No one complained about the snarl of abandoned open studs and trusses.
Sam Phillips was a young architect who had an operation that removed a brain tumor
And left him partially paralyzed and barely able to speak.
His daughter Susan,

A beautiful girl who made straight A's and played first-chair flute five years in a row,
Rolled his wheelchair around the block at sundown on mild evenings.
Her mother, Mary, was a librarian who parked her blue Hudson beside the alley.

It was a good neighborhood.

For a multitude of shameful reasons,
At a time when African Americans were going through hell elsewhere,
People in the twelve blue-collar homes in the 1700 block of Connection Road
Wrongfully went about their *own* business.
The deep, collective sorrow is,
They never thought about it,
And nothing can redo that.

Andrew grew into manhood elsewhere.
When he returned several years later,
All the houses were gone.
Stanchions and a barricade fence bore signs that read:
Keep Out, No Trespassing.
He parked,
Ignored the warnings,
Climbed the fence, and started on foot down what was once *his* street.
It was overgrown with wild sunflowers, tumbleweeds, and trash.
Clusters of sandburs filled the cracks and seams in the concrete.
Bindweed grew in a huge mound over a pile of partially burned tree stumps,
Bagworm cocoons hung on dead branches of a single wild juniper.
The former lots were indistinguishable from one another.
Nevertheless, he found the double slab on which he had scratched his name.
If he had had a masonry chisel,
He would have taken the *Eby Construction Co. 1950—I am Andrew* corner with him.
As it was,
He had to leave it.

Standing in the dry, hot wind,
He became acutely aware of grasshoppers and meadowlarks.
If he were to remain until after dark,
He knew there would also be lightning bugs, mosquitoes, and cicadas
... and maybe a full moon
Like the one on the night Roberta Slansky,
Stuck in her cottonwood tree swing,
Screamed, "Copperhead!"
And her mother chopped the wriggling thing
Into Vienna-sausage-size pieces with a hoe.

The cottonwood would have been over there,
A few yards beyond his bedroom window.
Many nights its rustling leaves mocked him
With the remnant of a kite his father had taken hours to make
From a yardstick, brown paper, and a strip torn from an old bedsheet for the tail.

He played right here with homemade rubber guns made from scrap wood
And half-inch-wide bands cut from old inner tubes.
It was a dodging, running game.
Each marksman had ten bands,
Each hit was a point.
The one with the most hits out of ten tries won the round,
The one with the most rounds when they decided to quit
Got to choose the next game.
Sometimes it was "Annie Annie Over"
—throwing a tennis ball over the roof to the unseen person on the other side.
If they caught it, they ran around either end of the house
To tag you before you could safely escape around to their side.
Each tag was a point,
Ten points was a game.
The winner got to choose the next game,
And so it went
On a block of Connection Road that now lays deep beneath a six-lane highway
Providing passage for thirty-three million vehicles a year to somewhere.

Crux of the Matter

Fervor left from yesterday
Isn't the memory,
Nor is it something new.
It is the intent in a progression of words
Marching one at a time across a page
To tell a story
Before the eraser and black line
Start their balanced pruning.

Taking Responsibility

Lincoln Elementary opened in 1885,
Was replaced with a new building in 1938,
And closed forever May 23, 2012.
It was on the corner of two of the busiest streets in town.

In 1947,
Children walked themselves to and from the school.
They went home for lunch
And were not afraid of strangers.

Some older children rode their bikes.
They carried things in saddlebags over the back fenders
And parked in playground racks.
The only losses were occasional padlock keys.

Drivers obeyed school zones better then than now,
Not because police officers were waiting to give them tickets,
But because they cared about setting good examples
As much as what they themselves were doing at the moment.

Police officers recorded license tag numbers
Of courteous drivers throughout the town for a weekly drawing.
It was a big deal to receive a silver license plate star from the police chief
And have your name announced on the radio.

Once a year a policeman came to school
To talk about perils and safety.
Long before alcohol and drugs became a problem,
Staying out of the street was the message of the day.

Children actually heeded advice they were given,
They laughed, and played, and horsed around to and from school,
They stayed on the sidewalks, walked their bikes across the intersections,
And no one worried.

Lifespan of a Newspaper Edition

People received news twice a day
From a canvas bag
Carried by a neighborhood paperboy
Who folded and tucked it into thirds
And threw it with precision onto their doormats.

It came in time for breakfast
And late afternoon to be discussed at the supper table.
Before bedtime,
What didn't line the cat's box or wrap the garbage
Ended up in an orange crate beside the washing machine on the back porch.

As an elementary school project,
Boys and girls pulled their wagons door to door
Once a week
Around square blocks of neighborhood sidewalks,
Collecting papers for the PTA.
When the big Saturday morning came,
A large stake-bed truck parked in the schoolyard.
Excitement prevailed along the waiting queue
As children and their parents off-loaded their stacks of papers.
Clean hands were quickly smeared with black ink.

If it was windy,
The driver stood on the truck bed beside the growing load
And attempted to contain stragglers with a green tarpaulin.
Children made a game of retrieving the lost sheets
That blew against the schoolyard fence.

Whether full or not, the truck left at noon.
At the shredder it was weighed, unloaded, and weighed again.
The PTA received a check in the following Tuesday's mail,
And a notice was posted outside the principal's office:
Thank you, everyone. The paper drive was a success.

At a nearby shipping dock, ribbons of the deconstructed news
Soon surrounded valuables en route to destinations otherwise safely
unattainable.

The abolished paragraphs lived on as indisputable facts:
"I remember seeing in the newspaper . . ."
Was common parlance of the day.

Clearly Understood

Sweaters were what we wore when our mothers were cold.
Work was what we did when our fathers meant business.
Learning to ponder the movement of clouds and the abundance of stars
Was what we did for ourselves, lying on our backs in the grass.

Open-Minded

I stood on the knoll an autumn day
As a sprightly wind preened the molting maples.

I cast a long shadow at four o'clock
And mused among the leaves that gathered there.

Pigeon House

Weeds adorn the empty building on all sides.
Along its dilapidated chain-link fence,
Faded red and white *Keep Out!* signs
Dangle from rusted pigtail wires.

It is too far to throw a rock,
But the windows are broken anyway,
And graffiti covering graffiti
Variegates the rough brick.

Of what use is an old elementary school
Where no one goes anymore,
On land whose alternative
Is a trashed vacant lot?

It would cost money to tear it down,
Money of which the city barely has enough
To provide swollen classes elsewhere
With standardized performance outcomes.

And so, the building attempts to bury itself.
This remnant of dignity,
That one day lay across an architect's drawing table,
Is now chagrined to endure disintegration.

If ruins have souls in another dimension of reality,
This old school is there in perpetual magnificence,
Having provided every child a desk, a Big Chief tablet,
And a three-thirty bell at the end of each day's discoveries.

Divorce

A firm wood-on-wood report
At ten past two
Finished the dirty work.

The magistrate and courtroom ancillaries shuffled out.
The attorneys whispered a moment to their clients,
Then snapped their briefcases shut.

In the aftermath,
Where the rubbish had been dumped,
The room fell silent.

Newly single people who left the façade through different doors
Immediately confronted the dazzling sun
With reflexive squinting.

Modern Complication

In the beginning,
Like the Great Story,
The personal story opens.
A time warp then receives life through its final emotions
To the ceremonial reading of the will.

This news sometimes surprises with joy,
Sometimes disappoints with anger,
And sometimes irreparably fractures relationships that linger.

The best plan,
When it works
—but not known for sure until it does—
Is when there are no surprises,
And the heirs deal in memories
While the lawyers deal in holdings.

In the parchment age
Such things started with the finality
Of a hammer smashing an egg.
"The *Last* Will and Testament . . ."
In India ink calligraphy on a large, single sheet
Recorded fate with a flourishing quill.

The sturdy document,
Folded into a paper sandwich,
Was tied with a black ribbon,
Intended,
Dickens-style,
Only to be opened
By a dour lawyer in waistcoat.
The formality alone
Signified invincibility.

Then came the mechanized age of silk stockings, steno pads, and Dictaphones.

Lawyers quickly adopted fluid oration
Into page upon page of contingencies and modifiers
Directly proportional in number
To advancements in typewriter technology.
Resulting documents became much thicker than parchment sandwiches,
More arcane,
And to the benefit of lawyers,
More litigious.

As governments plugged holes in regulations
With more regulations
—never with increased clarity or reduced size—
Probate lawyers ventured further into the protection business.

The folly in a trust agreement on today's table
Is one inch thick,
Averages 259 pages,
Weighs three-and-one-half pounds,
And has a table of contents with 408 headings.

How is it done?
With boilerplates,
The virtual namesakes of industrial physically protective walls
Between inside heated pressure
And outside ambience.
Lawyers electronically borrow limitless contingent possibilities
And craft them into sentences often running a hundred words or more
—sentences that include words like *co-agents named in the conjunctive,*
And hotchpot provision.

The soundest investment advice is the simplest:
"If you can't understand it,
Don't invest in it."
If only this applied to wills.

When a day comes to accept mortality,
The urge arises to consider placing a want ad:

"In search of attorney reputed to be good. Client aware of two types: (1) a ruthless, intimidating person indispensable in litigating circumstances, and (2) a humane intellect needed in present instance to record final wishes."

But a third alternative is how it works.

The end of the story
Is to be written before the end,
Not by the author,
But by a surrogate attorney with a vested interest
Not in the spirit of legacy
But in the possibility of defense . . .
Need it be said,
For a postmortem fee.

Surrogates draft wills with unctuous skill.
Their obsequious questions
Raise fear and doubt where none is perceived,
And convince clients to expect enmity,
To trust the legal version of a story
Inadequately understood,
And enter a witnessed signature
Beside an "x" at the bottom of the final page.

Way back before lawyers,
Entreaties were kept in oral tradition
—deviating and waning with the passage of time—
Nevertheless, preserved as needed to be.
Confronted with death,
If time allowed,
Assets passed from progenitors to heirs with a single word: "Here."
If the occurrence came as a gust from nowhere,
The communal fire was maintained later that night than usual,
And the day after was not disputed.

A Middle-Class Material Legacy

When the house was new,
Three rooms of apartment furniture
Were sparsely dispersed throughout six rooms,
And the double garage held just one car
That had never been parked overnight anywhere but on a street.
The new baby had a bedroom of his own
And a nice yard soon to be discovered.

Four years later he had a sister.
Slowly, silver, china, and crystal,
Inherited from deceased relatives,
Were diligently matched into service for twelve,
One or two pieces at a time,
Christmas after Christmas
—six settings of everything to be left to each child.

On a tight budget for years,
Instead of saving every surplus dollar,
Art and rugs were rationalized now and then
As being worth the money spent.
Of course, in terms of resale value, that was not true,
But the enjoyment was invaluable.
And enough money still got set aside for the future.

In the bedroom used as a study,
Two walls of bookcases were filled one book at a time,
Each remembered by content,
If not by title and author,
And recallable into service at a moment's notice.
There was a small executive desk, a computer desk,
A leather reading chair, and a sound system.

Now, beneath the cornice above the bookcases,
A ribbon of diplomas and certificates,
With seals and calligraphy difficult to read,
Is a record of endeavor,

Scrolled like the end credits of a movie
People leave in a dark theater
Before the soundtrack finishes.

CARRYOVER

It took the prosperous buyers an hour to sign the closing documents
And drive directly to their new old house.
While the children ran echoes up and down the stairs
Into hard-wall, bare-floor space,
Their parents and an architect went room to room
Taking pictures and making lists of changes
To rejuvenate the premises.

On the other side of town,
Blocks and blocks of apartments,
All the same,
Are closely stacked together,
Each unit with two or three windows,
Its own slot in a bank of mailboxes,
And a long list of rules and regulations posted inside a kitchen cabinet door.

Regardless of the place,
To grow up with a safe beginning
Is a precious virtue.
The wanderers,
Those who are deprived of the opportunity,
And those who have it all, but all is not enough,
Restlessly adapt until the day they can get away.

Outside the windows of their figurative escape train,
In the middle of nowhere,
Location is incidental.
Inside is a very different situation.
When a complete stranger sharing a table in the dining car asks,
"Where are you from?"
The question cannot be left hanging in the air.

At the Bottom of a Desk Drawer

It was like a ship in a bottle
Afloat upon the glass,
Twine drawn from a bobbin
Tying a kite to the ground,

Ink in a pen laying flat upon the desk
After risking the declaration,

Indistinct silhouettes in the reply envelope
Held to the light,

The beam of a headlight
Coming . . . passing . . . red,

The loneliness after leaving
The sidewalk at the corner.

Gloria,
You will never see this.

Oh, Boy

Stuck again
Dragging ink across pages
Soon crumpled and lobbed into the wastebasket.

Where is the patience
For the thread of a new idea
To crack this impasse?

Inspiration is difficult to explain,
Except to say,
Thank God for it.

Pride

Lugo came in a rusty old truck
Filled with tools, plastic barrels,
And a red power lawnmower.
As he scooted carryout lunch trash aside
For Jim to sit in the passenger's seat,
He addressed his new customer
With the appellation "Mister" Jim.

During the trip,
Lugo said he was born in the U.S.
Of parents who now lived in Mexico.
He had a two-year-old daughter.
He was Catholic and Republican.
Catholic was understandable,
Republican, Jim doubted, but accepted.

Gordon, the destination nurseryman,
Possibly early sixties,
With Santa Claus whiskers,
A loose ponytail secured with a string,
And faded, tie-dyed T-shirt and jeans,
Looked like what two generations back
Was called a hippie.

His faded wooden sign,
Propped askew inside the bent, rusted, chain-link fence read:
Fruit/Citrus Trees and Vines Since 1930.
Beyond it,
The nursery stock stretched in irregular rows
Through hundreds of trees potted in black plastic containers
Farther than could be seen.

At the widest part of the narrow muddy driveway,
Lugo parked on the left
Beside a hodgepodge of wet irrigation paraphernalia.
All the tree trunks were color coded with painted rings,

Nothing was marked with a price tag.
Gordon's one-man operation was simple:
Self-service at negotiated prices.

A Mexican man wanted to buy a bushel of limes.
Gordon told him in Spanish where to pick them.
An Anglo man was asking about orange tree varieties.
Gordon pointed him in a different direction.
Lugo asked for information about tangerines.
In a combination of English and Spanish,
He got a recommendation and directions.

Naïvely thinking a tangerine is a tangerine,
And that Lugo was with him for his muscle and truck,
It quickly became apparent,
He was Jim's agent.
Before they bought a tree,
They had to try the fruit,
Then negotiate a deal.

Variety to variety,
Lugo picked two tangerines at a time,
One for Jim, one for himself.
They checked how easy it was to peel the skins,
How much juice squirted out when they broke the segments apart,
How sweet and pulpy the fruit,
How large the seeds.

They verified for themselves and agreed,
Gordon's recommendation was good.
In the sales shack,
When Jim reached for his wallet,
Lugo pushed his arm away.
Not in Spanish, in English, he said,
"What's our discount?"

Gordon said, "Ten percent."
Lugo said, "Twenty."

Gordon said, "Fifteen."
Lugo again said, "Twenty."
Gordon looked Jim hard in the eye,
Jim looked at Lugo.
Gordon hesitated, then said, ". . . Twenty."

Lugo turned to Jim:
"I think you can use an orange tree and a lemon tree also."
"Where?"
"We will find a place."
Turning to Gordon he said,
"Twenty percent on two more?"
". . . Twenty percent."

The testing ritual was repeated
With the same result.
Gordon knew his citrus.
A cash transaction,
A pencil-written receipt,
And Lugo muscled three muddy barrels into his truck.
He said to Jim, "How did I do?"

On the trip home,
Trying hard to speak clear English,
He asked if Jim had children,
If he liked California,
If he liked the President.
Remembering Lugo was a Republican,
Jim said, "Yes, I am a Democrat."

They did not talk about immigration,
Or education,
Or healthcare,
Or welfare.
They talked about Mexican food,
How Lugo shinnied up tall palm trees to trim the tops,
And Lugo's brother in Mexico who had cancer.

Lugo pulled into a Quik Trip,
Prepaid inside,
And engaged Jim in steady, eye-contacting conversation
While he barely squeezed the pump handle,
Prolonging as long as possible
The flow of two-point-seven gallons
Into the gas tank.

"I need to mow a yard today,
Can I plant your trees tomorrow?"
"Of course."
After the trees were unloaded and he was gone,
A few blocks away,
Motorists passed a man siphoning gasoline
From a rusty old truck into a red lawnmower.

The Beach Hereabouts

A hundred yards beyond the bottom public access step
A sandpiper assiduously hunts midafternoon morsels
Beneath a blanket of sand trowelled back and forth by the tide.
As it chases and retreats along the scalloped edge,
Its shadow and reflection converge at its feet
Into a checkmark flickering over the continuously melting mirror.

On the incline of a nearby berm
A flock of seagulls—perhaps a hundred—rests in formation,
All facing southwest at the same angle to the sun.
Shadows of their white heads, gray bodies, and black-tipped tails
Proclaim *MY space* . . . *MY space* . . . *MY space* . . . *MY space* . . .
Like commas trailing through a contract yet to be written.

Gliding inches above the water
A brown pelican locks into the updraft from a chosen swell
By gently trimming the pitch of its seven-foot wingspan.
Hugging the crest of a breaking wave until the curl becomes turbulent,
With a single flap and slight twisting adjustment,
It veers seaward to make another choice.

Long strands from a kelp forest a mile out wash ashore
And the power that brought them in, unwilling to relinquish its hold,
Struggles to engulf them back.
Clinging as they go, the charcoal-like filigrees they drag into the wet sand ripples
Seem botanically equivalent to humanity attempting to communicate something
To an intelligence elsewhere in the galaxy.

Indeed it is natural to want, and tempting to envy,
Those whose fortunes allow them to have first-tier homes above the dunes,
With sight and sound of the ocean day and night.
Luckily, on the public beach below, with bare feet in squishy sand,
Extraordinary experiences, not possessable by anyone,
Are available to everyone.

In for a Penny, in for a Pound

Men and women . . . mostly men,
Swiveled on stools in Frank Redding's greasy spoon called The Coffee Cup.
They talked to one another and to the waitress with a starched napkin on her lapel
About what they read in the newspaper and thought of the weather.
The waitress kept their porcelain cups full of plain black coffee,
To which they added cream from small glass bottles and stirred with metal spoons.
When the cash register clinked, a dime changed hands.

Along came mass marketing.
Ambient jazz—by the way, the CDs you hear are for sale—
And aromas of gourmet beans—also for sale in bulk—
Have done for the coffee crowd what Bach and incense did for the Church.
People stand in line to choose from hundreds of possible pairings on the menu board,
Sit in an archipelago of soft chairs and at smooth wooden tables,
And lose themselves in technological purgatory:

> A college boy in a faded blue T-shirt,
> Whose sole transportation is a skateboard,
> Sits with a coiffed businesswoman who arrived in a red Mercedes convertible.
> He scribbles on a yellow pad
> And points to things on the screen of her notebook computer,
> Patiently teaching her what an executive is presumed to know
> And does not dare reveal to subordinates that she doesn't.

> On the other side of the room
> A girl not old enough for an adult driver's license
> Maneuvers her thumbs across a sheet of black glass
> In a trophy-cup NASCAR game.
> Beside her a boy who behaves like a boyfriend
> Is eager to take over
> And pit his driving skill against hers.

Two tables away, a thirty-something metrosexual
In five-hundred-dollar casual attire and a perfect three-day beard
Shows a chart on his phone to a retired couple in sweatshirts and sneakers.
The three of them are discussing something on which he is working
And in which their most recent ETF has holdings.
They smile at his enthusiasm.
He is astounded by how much they know.

Many of the people in the room are alone,
Alone with their computers and earphones,
Alone with their earphones and books,
Alone with their earphones and crossword puzzles:
The gentleman with a spreadsheet,
The woman searching to buy something on the web,
The barista on a break who texts her friends,
The entrepreneur whose business address is a post office box,
And whose office facility is a table in the corner.

No ceramic cups, saucers, or metal spoons here,
No waitresses, no conversations with strangers,
No free refills.
About ten percent of Americans eighteen years and older
Crave this twenty-first-century equivalent of The Coffee Cup.
Five dollars apiece they spend per visit is not an expense,
It is a ritual.

Shortest Month of the Year

Saturday without an agenda,
In jeans and sweatshirts,
Encircled with the February Southern California ocean breeze,
A family bought fish sandwiches from a sidewalk vendor
And found a place to use the seawall for a table.

One o'clock sun on the water
Laid a path of diamond-bright shimmer halfway to the horizon.
In both directions up and down the coast,
Four- and five-foot waves rolled ashore
In hypnotic thrashing that soothed away distractions from vehicles on the road.

A vintage biplane slowly towed a MetLife banner from the south.
Four pelicans effortlessly glided by in the opposite direction.
Three hundred yards out,
Packs of surfers bobbed like black cats seeking mouse holes.
One or two at a time pounced, peeled in, dropped, and paddled back out.
Many more unsuccessfully tried and tried again.

Grandmother said,
"We are lucky not to be in Boston now.
They had two and a half feet of snow last night,
And a foot more is falling today."
    She thought of forty-two years ago,
    When she and her husband lived there
    In an upstairs uninsulated apartment
    On the orange trolley line.
    Ice and hoarfrost built up inside the windows.
    Some Saturday nights they and their infant son
    —the man beside her now who cuddles *his* son—
    Snuggled in warm blankets on a sofa
    While listening to vinyl records in the dark.
    They often fell asleep before embers in the hearth had gone out.
    At the corner, once an hour,
    A trolley, usually empty,

Rumbled down Centre Street,
Clanging its bell in the quiet night.

A different year a huge nor'easter brought the city to a standstill
And confined them for a weekend.
They wore double sweaters to conserve heating oil,
Simmered a large pot of soup on the electric range
For humidity as well as aroma,
And for the fun of it,
Used a kerosene lamp until the kerosene was gone.
Then they used candles until they too were gone.
Outside the living room window
Snow fell through the mantle of light cast by the corner streetlamp
Like flakes swirling in an antique globe paperweight.
By the second morning, wind had turned the landscape
From variegated shadows
Into a confluent curvilinear luminance.
Snow continued to fall off and on all day Sunday.
Shoveling was nearly impossible, but he had to try.
She baked chocolate chip cookies and his favorite Cornish pasty.
Street plows came that night and covered everything back
Deeper than it had been before.
Monday morning . . .

Abruptly, her thought was interrupted
By a squadron of pelicans in V-formation directly overhead.
Her grandson saw them too; he reached up, and a smile crossed his face.
His mother and father paid little attention.
They were in a conversation
Comparing preacquaintance Vermont downhill skiing
With the Colorado Rockies and California Sierras.

> Grandfather was thinking about the difference
> Between the sixty-five-degree California February day by the ocean
> And a February Boston winter
> In the second-floor apartment
> Where he made a makeshift darkroom in a closet.

Unlike digital photography,
Every film-based exposure cost money,
So he rolled his own 35mm canisters
From bulk black-and-white film he purchased at Lechmere's in Dedham
And used Kodak chemistry to push as many exposures as possible
Into useable and occasionally artistic prints.

One of his favorite pictures
Was of a late-night orange-line trolley
Plowing into a blizzard
Before street crews had come to trench a canyon
And blow shoulder-high mesas onto both sides of the street.
Pelting horizontal snow
Eddied around large mounds
Of what a few hours earlier were parked cars.
Like frozen sparklers,
The hooded streetlights
Delineated a winding way into the distant realm of night.
There were no footprints or tire tracks.

Alone in the cold,
He stood in the middle of Centre Street
Between two quickly filling rail troughs
To capture a trolley's receding taillight
And crackling sparks from its overhead dragline.
In the darkroom he printed the result as a diptych.
The left panel was overexposed in high contrast,
The right, underexposed in low contrast.
He called it *Tomorrow*.

What's that? he thought.
His infant grandson, snuggling in the stroller beside him
Was also thinking, *What's that?*
It was acoustic guitar music rising from the beach below to the south.
A group of men, women, and children in white shirts
Had gathered near an old thatched hut.

If they were nearer,
The photo album they passed around
And the bowl of ashes
Would have been evident.
Each in turn accepted a wooden scoop,
Voiced a remembrance,
Took a portion from the bowl,
And cast it into the jumbling grit of a receding wave.

On the land side of the seawall above,
The family concluded their meal,
Stuffed their trash into a green barrel,
And looking ahead,
Ambled away on the sidewalk.
They did not notice the photographer behind
Who captured a long shot with no one else in the frame,
And a different shot of seventeen people, also with backs to the camera,
Standing at the surf's edge with heads tilted downward.

Back at his computer
He Photoshopped the images into a low- and high-contrast diptych
He titled *Henceforth*.

Stakeholders and Others

From many angles around the central plaza
Can be seen a class of inner-city second graders on a field trip,
Mingling among adult passersby.
Under protective teachers' eyes,
They eat sack lunches on the lawn
And frolic among the trees.
They are a random assortment of race, ethnicity, and gender,
And they are joyful.

Their code of conduct is spontaneously natural
Because they like each other:
    no need for an emphatic paragraph
    embedded within a signed contract,
    that holds in check as much as legally possible
    prejudice and indifference in a workplace.
The only rules that need enforcement
Are for safety and to curtail innocent mischief.

Hezekiah Thomas was such a child.
He grew to manhood within strict social limitations,
Then persevered to become a member of the first black union in the country,
The Brotherhood of Sleeping Car Porters.
On June 15, 1937,
As a Pullman car attendant during the apex of luxurious rail travel,
He was aboard the inaugural coast-to-coast run of the Santa Fe Super Chief.
It was America's premier cross-country train.

After riding it nine thousand miles a week
For twenty-five impeccable years of "Yes, sir," and "Yes, ma'am" with a broad smile,
He retired.
His Social Security and railroad pension checks provided him adequate income,

But after his wife died, needing something to do with his time,
He became the houseman for a socialite purveyor of fine antiques to her peers.
In a starched white jacket and black bowtie,
He answered her door and telephone, chauffeured her Rolls-Royce,
And in white gloves, served her afternoon callers sherry from a silver tray.

He was elite among his peers.
Across town,
Grandparents of many of the second-grade students on the central plaza today
Were living in the inner-city themselves.

Some things have changed since then.
In 1971 the Super Chief was removed from service for lack of customers;
Only the wealthiest have servants,
And commendably,
Maybe not everywhere,
But here—today at least—
The central plaza is a bustling place
Joyous among a group of second graders
Whose opportunities are on the line.

Small Business

A block behind establishments lining both sides of the busy north-south thruway
Are four small businesses in a late-mid-century building without a canopy.
The façade trim is painted a somewhat ghastly yellow-tan.
A concrete parking lot abuts the sidewalk along the flat storefronts.

One merchant sells cigarettes, spirits, and lottery tickets.
Next door, a vacuum-cleaner store sells and repairs sweepers,
And rents carpet-cleaning machines displayed on the sidewalk.
Third, a jeweler with a few rings, necklaces, and bracelets in two glass display cases
Derives most income from repairing similar items and replacing watch batteries.
The fourth shop is Verl's Alterations.

Five miles away is a one-stop megamall
With acres of three-tier parking,
Abundant quantities of everything offered,
And continuous 10%-or-More-Off sales.
People travel there in droves to *shop*.
Never mind if individual stores come and go
Those that remain must continuously pursue a "fresh" look
Because a few doors away
Is plenty of competition.

Verl was once a tailor in haute couture
At the quintessential department store in the heart of downtown.
In a series of customized visits,
He measured men and boys from neck to toe,
Created patterns and revised basted skeletons of their suits,
And had at least one or two more precision adjustment fittings
Before delivering the final garments.
Proud new owners took their suits home interleaved in tissue paper
Packed in sturdy white boxes.

Eventually the store was sold and consolidated into a mass-market fleet.
Thereafter, all men's clothes were sold off the rack.

Verl was assigned to pinning alterations.
The required sewing was done at a regional location.
Customers no longer knew his name . . . or cared to.
They simply paid a surcharge for a required service
And returned for their goods in two weeks.

One day he saw *For Rent* in the window of a 225-square-foot empty storefront.
He thought, *Why not? Why not give it a try?*
So he did.
He was still doing alterations,
The difference was,
He was doing them for people who recognized his commitment,
Not people who took what he did for granted.

Forty years later he is eighty
And still at it in the same place.

•

"This is Gregory Cordeem. I am standing outside the Spangler Center Auditorium at Harvard University, where three small-business operators selected at random by the Better Business Bureau from its 400,000 U.S. members have just participated with Bill Gates and Warren Buffett in a forum on the ethics of capitalism in a free-market economy.

Verl Drazper is one of those three people.
He is an alteration tailor from Terre Haute, Indiana.

"Mr. Drazper, was it intimidating sitting with the two richest people in the world?"

"No. Before we went on stage, Mr. Gates smiled from ear to ear when he shook my hand. He raised his right leg at an angle in front of me and said, 'Is this a good cuff?'
Mr. Buffett said, 'Verl, it's good to meet you. Back in Omaha, I may have a couple of old shirt patterns in the basement. Would you like to have one?'"

"How did that make you feel?"

"At ease. Then all of us took a bottle of water from the same cooler."

"Did Mr. Gates and Mr. Buffett give you a chance to talk, and did they listen to what you had to say?"

"Yes and yes."

"What did you learn from them?"

"That everybody is special."

"What do you mean by that?"

"A lot of people work hard. A few are incredibly more successful and a lot more fortunate than the rest of us, but we all need the same amount of air every day no matter who we are."

"That sounds very philosophic. Explain what you mean."

"Son, I charge six dollars to put cuffs in a pair of pants like you've got on. That's three times what it was when I went into business for myself forty years ago. During those years my rent has gone up three times more than that.
I have put five girls through college.
My wife and I own our own home.
I buy a four- or five-year-old car every five years or so.
I have traveled a lot of places throughout the country and a few abroad.
I walk a mile or two four or five times a week.
I eat what I want; I love ice cream.
I follow the Broncos, the Royals, and the Lakers.
I sleep well at night,
Go to church on Sunday,
Read the *New York Times* every day on my computer,
Keep track of my ETFs,
Read mystery stories,
And sit on my patio warm evenings,
Or in front of my fireplace on cold nights,
And drink a cup of coffee or a glass of wine.
But son, do you know what really keeps me going?"

Knocked off guard because Verl has gone silent, Gregory Cordeem stands there like a statue.

"Mr. Drazper.
. . . Mr. Drazper?"

"What, son?"

"Are you okay?"

"Of course I'm okay!"

"You were telling me about what I presume was dialogue you had with Mr. Gates and Mr. Buffett."

"I know I was."

"Why did you stop?"

"I was waiting for you."

"Me? Why? This is your story."

"I asked you a question and I am waiting for your answer."

"Uh . . . what do you want me to say?"

"Do you know what keeps me going?"

"No, I don't."

"Well, then, let me ask you a different question:

What gets *you* up in the morning?"

"Come on! My alarm clock."

"No, I'm serious. What gets you up in the morning?"

"Mr. Drazper, this interview is *not* about me, and we only have a little bit of time left."

"Exactly! We only have a little bit of time left!

It is not about how great or how seemingly unimportant our knowledge and skills are.
It is that everybody benefits from nice cuffs in their pants
And a comfortable waist.
That's what keeps me going.
Someday you may be first anchor of this TV station, CEO of its nationwide network,
A beekeeper who sells home-bottled honey at a farmer's market,
Or an author who writes children's books in an Orlando condominium.
The important thing that keeps us *all* going,
Is to be happy with what we do to help other people."

"That's it?"

"That's it.
. . . and now aren't you supposed to say,
'This is Gregory Cordeem reporting live from Harvard University.'"

Chance of a Lifetime

A crisp, clear morning with Indian summer sun rising against their backs
Bade them to enjoy one of the last outdoor opportunities of the season.
He and his daughter-in-law selected a patio table overlooking the small runway.
A Cessna passed overhead and landed a half mile below the hill.
His grandson, in hat, sweater, and blanket, slumbered unaffected by the noise.

"Have you ever flown out of here on a commuter flight to Las Vegas?"

"Once."

"Is it nonstop?"

"Yes. I did it two years ago to see Mom and Dad when they were well."

After a silent lapse, another small single-engine plane went over.
The baby stirred but did not wake.
Their coffee, as a means of facilitating conversation, had barely cooled enough to sip.
He reticently looked at the boy,
At the repeating line of runway strobes,
And then back at his daughter-in-law.

"Have you thought about going to see your mother again?"

"Yes, but I am nursing and I can't leave Davy."

"Why not take him with you?"

"Oh no! I can't do that. I don't want him exposed to the germs in the nursing home."

In the absence of ensuing conversation, she was thinking:

> *Daddy went to the hospital for surgery, and should have been home in a week. Instead he was dead by then from septicemia he caught in the hospital. Mom's diabetes is bad, but the care home does what she needs and we can talk on the phone.*

Her father-in-law was remembering forty-five years ago:

I had seen Dad twice in ten years.
It was not an acrimonious separation,
He liked to fish, and I was moving around the northeast.
After Mom died he sold everything and moved south to the Gulf.

We had good intentions of maintaining contact,
But when news of things we were doing became stale and repetitive,
We never seemed to make time to exchange letters about our ideas and feelings.
The decade intervened one day at a time.
Nine months after the last Christmas card,
I splurged on a person-to-person telephone call
To introduce him to the voice of a girl with whom I had fallen in love.
He wished us well and had very little to say about himself;
If he was in pain, I did not know.

Before the month was out, I got a call.
It was a young doctor with a gentle, imploring voice:

> "Your dad told me you were his son. He did not ask me to call you, I took it upon myself... I know the two of you have not communicated for a long time, but he is proud of you. He is very sick and does not have long to live. Can you come to see him?"

My new part-time job, a nearly empty checkbook, a scheduled graduate thesis defense coming up, and the very weekend I was going to propose marriage were reasons I gave myself for not leaving immediately.

A day or two after the call, Dad died in a hospital with no one in the chair beside him to hold his hand.

I will forever regret it, and his forgiveness is beyond recovery.

He was the dad who held my hand as a toddler to help me walk, sat me on his lap and held my hands on the steering wheel as together we guided the car. He held the back of my bicycle seat until I could pedal and balance myself. He bought me a fielder's glove and taught me how to catch flies and pick up grounders, handed me Grapettes from a circulating ice-water machine on hot summer days, and hugged me while an emergency room doctor, without anesthesia, burned away impetigo-infected mosquito bites on my legs and arms with silver nitrate.

. . . She has to know this is her mother's eleventh hour.

How can I tell her she must go to Nevada now, and take her mother's grandson with her?

Diabetes is not an infection.

Moreover, the biological risk in nursing homes is to residents receiving germs brought in from outside not from contagion diaphanously lurking behind every door to worm into visitors' defenseless bodies.

Quite the contrary, the true peril is broken-heart disease caused by isolation.

It hastens the demise of residents and implants lingering shards of guilt into the hearts of loved ones who have failed to come forth.

A corporate jet screamed overhead and broke the meditative silence.
This time Davy woke up crying.
His mother picked up the boy and cuddled him with gentle whispers.
People seated at a nearby table observed a gentleman rise,
Put one hand on the woman's shoulder and the other on her infant son.
They did not hear him say, "I would like for you to go to Las Vegas,"
Or her reply: "Let me think about it."

Chill

Colorado sun
At a low angle
Skids across the forest floor
And speckles a woodpile
With feathers of light
For a chipmunk's warm breakfast.

Two hours later on a New York clock,
Yet the same moment in time,
Sun is yet to reach the street
Or the homeless man
Who huddles with an empty cup
Near a subway.

7:30 A.M.

Beside the computer and a photograph of him and their children,
She puts her daily Starbucks and a stack of papers on the desk.
At the bottom of the papers is her diary.
Often superseded, as it will be today,
She puts it back in her purse
And sits down to study overnight data before an eight o'clock briefing ahead.

A distracting thought comes to her about the day she started the diary.
It was the day after she first heard his voice across a room six years ago.
So much has happened since then . . .
Abruptly, her desk phone rings.
Whoever it is says, "Sorry, wrong number," and hangs up,
Leaving her with a dial tone and the eight o'clock briefing.

Least Common Denominator

Is life a protoplasmic carrier of spirits
Through the isthmus of a cosmic hourglass,
A closed system of sacred granules
Passing finitely between two infinite realms,
One grain at a time,
Pulled along by a mysterious gravity?

Shoreline Watercolors

Against the planet's spinning and winds

And the persistent tug of the moon,
Intermolecular forces hold together
The common, heaving ocean
Anchored nearly seven miles deep
In the Mariana Trench.

Rising from the west
Onto the Southern California coast,
Like jelly coming to a boil
At the rim of a caldron,
Each wave expends its last ounce of energy
To climb the shore.

Inevitably it loses its grip and falls back,
Clawing ripples in the sand.
The receding curtain of achromatic variegations
Undulate and glisten
Into a foamy bas-relief depiction
Of the mountains it scaled to get here.

The First Two Opportunities of a Day

Windows were open,
The sky was overcast,
Birds awoke an hour before water began flowing in the garden fountain.

"Good morning," Margaret said, rolling toward Sam,
"How did you sleep?"
"I was restless; how did you sleep?"
"Very well. Did you have a peaceful night?"
"Ha, ha, ha . . . I said I was restless!"
"Pardon me, please, for putting you on."
"Ha, ha, ha. Does that mean what I think it means?"
"Ha, ha, ha, ha." Margaret laughed so hard she farted.
"Oops. Puffy the Dragon there!"
"Ha, ha, ha, ha. I couldn't resist."
"Ha, ha, ha, ha, ha."

Presently,
—well, not quite presently—
But after a while,
They left the house.

Their Labrador on an extended leash,
Probed obscure scents in the vegetation,
Peed here and there,
And scratched hardily.

His defecation scooped with a doggie mitt
Was discarded into the trailside receptacle.
His leash was drawn closer,
The long walk began.

A mile underway,
A woman in her sixties approached.
She appeared to be of relaxed means:
Somewhat thin,
Black slacks,

A black-and-white striped jersey,
Salt-and-pepper hair gathered into a loose bun.
She had a leash in each hand.

Her pugs veered toward the Lab,
Friendship was explored
Fore and aft.
Amid the oscillating tails,
Sam stooped and offered a supine hand.

"Mr. Peabody likes everybody,
Ms. Penny prefers to keep to herself."

The lady brushed a wisp of hair behind her ear and continued,
"Is your Lab a rescue dog?"

"Yes, he was abandoned."

"He is a beautiful dog."

"Thank you."

"These dogs are my son's.
He raised Mr. Peabody from a pup.
Ms. Penny is missing an eye,
I don't know what happened.
He got her at a dog park.
Her owners took her there,
Intent upon returning home without her.
Both dogs stay with my son's girlfriend.
But she doesn't have much time to walk them,
So, I come by and take them out."

Mr. Peabody lunged into Sam's lap
And swiped a kiss across his mouth and nose.

"Ha, ha."

Ready to leave,
Ms. Penny paced at the limit of her leash.

Sam rose.
The small talk finished,
Yet seemed unfinished.
He lingered in slight awkwardness.

The woman mentioned her son again.
"He is in Afghanistan.
They," nodding toward Mr. Peabody and Ms. Penny, "and his girlfriend
Will be glad when he comes home."

A silence followed.

Margaret broke in: "You will be, too."

Sam added, "Hopefully it won't be long.
Thank you for his service."

More silence.

Furtively nudging a pull from their Lab,
The couple turned, Sam saying, "Okay, Mr. Cheerio."

Margaret said, "I hope you have a good day."

The woman answered, "Thank you, you too."

While the three people
And three dogs had stopped there,
It was night in Afghanistan.

Without a Choice in the Matter

I turned out the bedside lamp,
And opened the curtain.
Clouds in the north cast back the glow
Of midnight solitude in the village beyond.

Upon raising the window a couple of inches,
A cool, damp breeze slightly fluttered the note tablet
I keep handy to record fleeting thoughts
That sometimes come to me in the night.

Getting into bed between soft flannel sheets
Topped with a warm blanket,
I rolled on my side toward the window
And hermetically sealed a cocoon around myself.

As I relaxed and listened to a gentle drizzle upon the trees,
My imagination drifted in thought to a dark April night
In the cold North Atlantic,
Far, far away from home.

Those with wealth traveled for pleasure,
And could hear the sea swishing along the hull beneath their open portholes.
The others, in windowless compartments, enduring incessant engine noise,
Were traveling in pursuit of new and better lives.

During four nights on a calm sea,
Protected by inch-thick steel walls,
They all relaxed beneath warm blankets
And slept soundly.

From the richest to the poorest,
Their days were filled with solitary and community opportunities
To reflect on the journey and anticipate reaching Pier 59 in New York City.
After all, it was the maiden voyage of the largest ship in the world!

Sunday at 11:30 p.m.,

The fifth night of continuing calm water,
The invincible titan that carried them
Sped along at nearly maximum speed.

Ten minutes later,
Seemingly out of nowhere,
A crystal saber appeared
And grazed the titan's side.

She stumbled to a halt
And bled two hours, forty minutes
Before falling to the ground
12,600 feet below.

Survivors rescued from her lifeboats
Told of noble, heroic deeds
Among those who were left
To draw upon their ultimate courage.

Outside my window
The drizzle had turned to rain.
I pulled the covers tighter
And lay there safe, dry, and warm.

It agonized me to think,
Yet it was impossible not to,
I would not have been in a lifeboat that night,
I would have succumbed to the frigid sea in the darkness.

I wrestled with the horrible thought.
No, no!
I would not have done it with courage.
I would have been a trembling coward.

Then I thought,
If sometime before the fact those brave souls had lain in warm beds,
And conjectured what they would do if something like this happened to them,
They might have felt the same as I felt.

I reached for my notepad and wrote in the darkness:

> Beyond reason,
> Courage is something we may have
> And not know it until we need it.

Hypothetical Omniscience

Another book is out
About near death,
In a body maintained by machines,
While a conscious experience occurred
From an under-place
Into multidimensions
Coursing through a cosmic heart.

If a Big Bang began it all,
Reality in four dimensions
Is an introspective awareness
Of length, width, height, and time.
The newest, nearest, and smallest things in the universe
Might merely be different expressions of
The oldest, largest, and farthest.

Perhaps the entire system
Is a set of entities like nesting matryoshka dolls:
Approximately 200 billion atoms in the human genome,
At least 100 trillion cells in the human body,
More than 10^{22} stars in the universe.
Awareness at any magnitude in these systems
Would not know the identity of the immense form of which it is a part.

However, it could discover smaller and smaller pieces of itself,
Eventually arrayed into proximate energy fields,
In which it would be impossible to decipher
One thing from another,
A level at which
An observer's own energy particles cannot be separated
From those being observed.

In another dimension,
Perhaps the fifth,
We *know* we are alive
With cosmic stitching of *us* to our protoplasm,

But *why?* remains a question.
Why have we momentarily been plucked out of an eternal realm
Into a region of free-will good and evil?

Since we have no equivalent accounts
Of before-birth experiences
To compare with near-death experiences,
Who knows?
We are perhaps an experiment
Conducted by eternity
To learn what we think of ourselves.

Approval Rating

He opened the sunroof
To let in the breeze
And freshness of morning en route.
When he arrived
And parked beneath a tree for shade,
His greyhound stood on the console,
Poked his long neck out,
And saluted the sky with five quick sniffs
And a snort.

Inch and a Half Rain

After a violent beginning,
Lightning and thunder
Occasionally grumble within stalled clouds
High in the atmosphere.

Strands of water pearls drip from the eaves,
And the bloom of crystal spheres
On the tips of pine needles
Glints in the gray midday light.

Here and there, the spheres drop,
Pft . . . pft . . . pft,
And invisibly poke through pungent humus
Into the woodland floor.

Water slipping over rocks and boulders
Trickles into cracks
And puddles around the bases
Like miniature moats.

It is apparent
The storm will linger into night
And cloud cover will continue to limit the view
From the empty chair by the window.

As the land saturates,
A better thing to do
Is take a chair beside the fire
And read.

Also with You

Peace is not a binary system.
It is a fading in increments
Between black and white
Of a thousand shades of trust
That liberate us from fear.

Indeed!
The gavel banged and a collector bought a $170 million painting,
While 400 million Chinese and 850 million Indians
Live on less than $2 per day.
In a different era
Slaves heard a similar sound,
And that too was final.
These disproportionate inequalities are difficult to comprehend
Over a glass of wine with friends in a well-appointed living room.
Nevertheless, repeatedly posing the tough question
Keeps the ignored answer alive:
If I don't value you, why do I expect you to value me?

God gives us the ability to think;
Yet in our quest for knowledge,
The mystery of knowing why
Is like discerning silhouettes from shadows
In a world of blazing color.

Twice

Beyond the help of medication,
With a small needle, her soul drifted away
Like a dandelion globe gently blown into a thousand umbrellas
Riding still air out of sight.

She may have been an older dog than she seemed,
Born and loved for years with another name,
Then somehow thrust into surviving by herself on city streets
With traffic, predators, puppies, foul food, and black water.

Her soft gray coat grew ratty;
The happy bark that welcomed someone home
Became a mean, high-pitched menace,
As she rapidly clawed the pavement to avoid danger.

One day she trusted against her instinct,
Found a snare around her neck,
Was cleaned, medically cared for,
Put on display, and had a new family.

She answered to a new name,
Had a safe bed and good food,
And someone to take her to a dog park
In a car in which she loved to ride.

Now, the noise without sound
Lingers inscrutably real,
Like noise gone silent in the earlier time
Hurt someone else.

Beyond Reason

July 8 he died of a lung cancer
He should not have had
Because he never smoked.
Life throughout its midst is a notion of

    What it is
        that begins and ends in energy and molecules,
        uniquely existing for a blink in an indefinable dimension
        with more than seven billion other people
        —twice as many as at his birth in 1960—
    In which we
        somehow aware of being alive,
        able to think
        and learn what is good from what is not,
        collectively bumble along and
    Have the opportunity
        to experience love
        like light reflecting from specks of dust,
        unseen before and after,
        but visible long enough during its happening
    To realize there is no such thing as nothingness.

Light of Day

Did a teenager in need of attention
At a church-group campfire
Spin a tale of when she was seven
That became a brushfire
Safer to let burn
Than admit to arson?

Divergent Aftermath

Behind tall, slender windows
Below blinking lights at the top,
Normal people within comfort zones
Did what they did every day,
More likely than not
Taking the beacon for granted.

On a Tuesday they boarded elevators
That safely conveyed them upward
Into the citadel's compartments.
Then the elevators, the windows,
The beacon, and the normal people
Became indistinguishable rubble.

Fourteen years have passed.
It is Martin Luther King Day.
It is Monday.
Around the world,
Who knows what prevails in the deepest realms of human thought?
We dare not take beacon light for granted anymore.

July 4

Across a wide ocean,
Beyond a king, Parliament,
Splendor, and courtly manners,
The obligation of submissive participation
Mutated into self-determination.

Seedpods sown by new, free wind
In the hither, unpretentious place,
Germinated into responsibility
Of ordinary people
For common good—or loss.

Night Light

The American two-party system—
a theoretically noble political arrangement,
with two sides to an argument,
and attainable substantive compromises—
Worked in the past.

The next Congress will be in session 110 days.
If the opposing side from either perspective continues always to be wrong,
And the expounding side from either perspective is presumed always to be right,
All 255 days of recess will be required
To schmooze the electorate into gullible support.

Who knows
What headlights are on in the dark?
It may be lobbyists and political action couriers
Delivering influence money, vote-control instructions,
Or scandalous campaign concoctions.

Alternatively better,
I would like to think the lights are honorable politicians
Who work late in the common good,
Making their way home
Through unlit neighborhoods.

Tangible Image of an Unknown Thought

Mid-December rain falls on Waterman Street
In the heart of a place
That tomorrow morning will draw a hundred thousand people out of bed
To make, manage, and spend money before closing out the year.

In the emptiness at 2:00 a.m.
Strings of holiday lights and tinsel
Glint and rustle in gusts that whip sheets of water
Across the canyon floor.

It looks as though a painter high in the night above
Is spilling solvent down a thousand dark windows
That bleed color mixed with silver
Onto the variegated plaza below.

An occasional taxicab or police car throws a wake several feet into the air
And once an hour an empty city bus passes like a middle-aged barge.
From an office five stories above
Someone is looking out a lighted window.

In what kind of task is the person engaged
That requires a push through the cold, miserable night to complete by morning,
From which a diversion has been taken
To stare upon incredibly lonely beauty no one else sees?

Bookending an Extraordinary Interim

Anticipating it for months,
They arose two hours early
To be fifty miles east and headed north before sunrise.
As it was,
They got underway half an hour late,
Drove a few blocks directly into the sun,
Then chose a twenty-minute coffee break in preference to an accident.

A thousand miles of discipline later,
They opened the cabin door
And another autumnal vacation
Unfolded into time as close to perfect
As they could imagine—
    unfettered from keeping track
    until the last possible moment.

Dawn on the day of return
Was fraught with exaggerated activity
In an attempt to suppress thinking about twenty-four hours earlier,
When the bedroom windows were open,
A leisurely breakfast was an hour yet to come,
And drawers and closets held clothes yet to be separated
    Into things left behind and things to be taken back.

Now they were saying out loud in unison,
"Good-bye, cabin in the woods."
In the rearview mirror,
Dust rolled behind the car
Until they reached the highway stop sign.
There, the accumulated whirl passed straight on in a dissipating cloud
As they turned to the right and headed home.

Lost Welcome

It began with a few flakes.
Some hit bare ground and instantly melted,
Others fell in the grass
And stacked upon themselves.

As a lace began to form,
The wind picked up
And soon swarms of needlelike grains
Were pelting in horizontal sheets.

The prolonged momentum
Piled drifts around everything in its way,
Cast plumes off the eaves,
And carved out craters along the lee side of the house.

By 3:00 a.m. it was over.
The clouds lifted,
The wind died,
And deep space sucked away the temperature.

In the subzero night without a moon,
Stars illuminated the emptiness
With enough glow to discern contours
Of every blanketed object in the yard.

When morning broke with brilliance,
A cardinal glided out of the east.
Unsuccessfully searching for the birdfeeder,
In a glint he was gone.

I wish I could have summoned him back.
It made no difference how many times I had left seed there before,
This time, when he needed it most,
I had failed him.

Think Before Taking Over a Large Yard

The mistake,
    moving from a city Cape Cod with a small English garden
    to a suburban prairie-style ranch house on an acre,
    was presuming the yard care would be the same.

The sellers,
    inside people to whom advantage of a large lot
    was privacy and the appearance of success,
    left management of their entire yard to elderly Clarence—
    taciturn, intransigent Clarence.
    When *Clarence interviewed Dean*,
    before extending the privilege of his service,
    he said, "No flowers, vines, or ornamentals,
    just grass, shrubbery, and trees,
    plain and clean."

Thursday mornings all summer,
    Clarence backed a former U-Haul box truck he had painted dark blue
    into the driveway,
    raised the back door,
    pushed out an old, thirty-six-inch power mower
    he walked behind with the seeming agility of a younger man,
    and cut his diamond-pattern signature into the grass.

Mid-October, the lawn went dormant and the final autumn leaves were mowed away.

When spring began anew,
    Dean's temptation to spade and plant the ground was too great to resist.
    Fulfillment of his weakness brought swift, crushing rebuke
    when Clarence came for his first mowing of the season.
    He knocked at the door.
    "I won't deal with flowers!"
    Lana said, "I will tell Dean."
    Next Thursday he knocked again.
    "If the flowers remain, I won't be back."
    Again Lana said, "I will tell Dean."

The third week,
 a few flowers had been moved to pots on the terrace,
 the rest had been given or thrown away.

Back in his comfort zone,
 Clarence contentedly mowed his diamond pattern
 as clean as a military haircut.

Mid-August his lawnmower broke.
 The repair shop told him parts were no longer available;
 that was why City Parks and Recreation
 scrapped the mower in the first place.
 As stubborn in his ways about the means
 as he was in what he would and would not do,
 he refused to buy a riding mower.
 Instead, the narrower swath his new push mower made
 required ten percent more passes,
 and ten percent more time,
 for which he wanted ten percent more money.

Dean complied,
 as did Clarence's other customers,
 but not his doctor:
  "Clarence, you are eighty-three years old.
  Your knees and back are giving you trouble.
  Get a riding mower or stop mowing."
 He stopped mowing.

Mr. Lee cut the grass in simple, straight rows.
 After the dormant winter,
 April came again.
 Ironically, he encouraged Dean to add flowers and ornamentals.
 The June result was magnificent.
 Dean thanked him with a sizeable bonus check.
 Mr. Lee smiled broadly and almost danced with joy.
 "As a young boy I fled the Khmer Rouge in Cambodia.
 I know nothing of my family.
 Twenty years I have saved for the day I could return.

Now I have the money to do it."
Like a hot air balloon silently suspended and cooling
when its burner flame is extinguished,
he slacked into thought.
Tears began to well.
Far too insufficient for an expression of his heart,
he could barely form the words, *"Thank you."*
After a moment he blinked,
redirected his gaze toward Dean, and murmured,
"I will find you someone else."

Mr. Tran had been a well-to-do pharmacist in Da Nang
with gardeners of his own.
In the United States the venerable émigré
was the patriarch of more than a dozen people
who lived together in a small rental house
on the other side of town.
He worked slowly,
required extra time,
and did a good job.

He, and other adults in the family
who spoke enough English to find work,
were dropped off and retrieved at various sites
in an old white station wagon
by the strongest young buck of the lot,
who spent the rest of his time hanging out with similar slackers.

Whether this activity got him into difficulty with the law
or with his associates was not clear.
The girl and a woman who came to collect Mr. Tran's check
said the buck and some of the family,
including Mr. Tran,
had left town the prior Friday.

Geronimo had quit a local beef processing plant job
and started Four Seasons Lawn Service
with his teenage son and one hired man.

They provided mowing and edging for a flat fee;
anything else was an à la carte charge.

By November he had a trailer,
   a riding mower with a grass-bagging attachment,
   a leaf vacuum for fall,
   and a snow blade for winter.

By spring he had a second pickup,
   a second crew,
   and more equipment.

He then lowballed his competition,
   wrenched several golf-villa lawns away from their long-term keepers,
   and substantially raised charges to his existing customers
      for the same work he now called *prestigious* service.
"Good-bye, Geronimo."

Dean was getting his hair cut
   when he joined a conversation
   between the adjacent barber and his customer
   about fairly priced lawn service.

The barber shared Dean's interest with other customers,
   and four days later,
   a red pickup hauling a ramp-gate trailer
   moseyed down the street and came to a stop.

Behind the windshield,
   a Raiders cap, aviator sunglasses, and the bridge of a nose
   peered beneath the top of the steering wheel.
   Then the man slowly emerged
   and walked like a bulldog to Dean's door.
   He did not speak English,
      gave no surname,
   just "Victor,"
   and a cell phone number.
   A single nod without a handshake
   concluded the exchange.

Thursday next,
   the pickup moseyed down the street again
   and coasted to a stop at the curb.
   Five-foot Victor, in the Raiders cap and sunglasses,
   slowly swaggered to the house
   for advance payment in cash
   —the only form of payment he would accept—
   before nodding back toward the truck.
   Two men got out,
   unloaded their things,
   and went to work.
   Slowly returning to the truck,
   Victor checked the next address in his pocket notebook,
   got in,
   and drove away to unload another crew.
   After a while he returned,
   waiting inside the air-conditioned cab
   for Dean's job to be finished.

The following week at the cash exchange,
   Dean gestured to Victor to have his men trim away small ivy runners
   beginning to overgrow the sidewalk beside the front door,
   and remove pine needles a recent wind had blown there.

When Victor and his crew were gone, so was the ivy.
   It had taken years to fill the space
   and climb the tree in the center.
   It was what visitors admired
   while waiting for the doorbell to be answered.
   Whacked away with a filament edger,
   nothing remained but short, leafless twigs.

Scarcely able to speak upon getting a phone recording,
   Dean left a message for Victor to call him immediately.
   No response came before Dean and Lana went to bed at 11:00 p.m.
   They discovered in the morning that in the night they had visitors.
   Wilted sprigs of ivy were plugged like a hair transplant.

Dean pulled one out and found it had no roots;
it was just a clipping.
Despite more attempts to reach him,
Victor never called back.

The next week when the red truck approached,
    Dean was waiting in the yard.
    Victor coasted to a stop and lowered the curbside window
    to hear Dean yell,
    "Get out of here or I will call the police!"
    At the word *police*, slow Victor came to life.
    He revved the engine, gnashed the transmission,
    and sped away as he yelled back in perfect English,
    "All it needs is water!"

Dean let Indian summer trail into autumn.
    He rented a mower twice,
    cut the grass himself,
    and ignored everything else.

The ivy patch did not recover.

Mid-April,
    freshmen football players
    put a flyer in the screen door:
    Good mowing service—a team effort—a fair price.
    Dean subscribed,
    and service was conscientiously delivered
    until the first week of August,
    when the coach took over their lives
    and quashed the entrepreneurial enterprise.

Sears was having a sale on lawnmowers.
    Dean bought a riding model with a bagging attachment.
    He donned goggles and a facemask,
    and called Lana into the yard to watch him get underway,
    as though he were driving a new car.
    In a quick hour the job was finished.

Bags of clippings were tied and stacked at the curb
for the Waste Management truck.
The mower was washed and garaged
. . . and Dean was having a catastrophic respiratory allergy attack.
After the same outcome the second week,
he scrapped his do-it-yourself plan
and sold the contraption from the parking lot of a nearby gas station.

"Hello, is this Southwest Nursery?"
"Yes."
"To whom am I speaking?"
"Liz."
"I notice your ad in the phone book says you plant and maintain flowers and trees.
Do you also do lawns?"
"Yes."
"Could you come by and give me an estimate?"
"Yes."

Liz, a country-girl graduate of a horticulture and turf program
at a state land-grant college,
came, clipboard in hand,
in a glistening gray pickup.
She and Dean walked the property
and came to an agreement.
She would plant and tend flowers herself;
Max, an employee, would mow the lawn.

Max followed through.
Liz, on the other hand,
showed up every few days with something else:
a flat or two of flowers,
a bag or two of cottonseed husks,
potting soil, mulching bark, more plants.
On and on,
one month,
two,

the job was never finished,
the bills were never itemized.
Even after a couple of discussions,
the situation did not improve.

"Hello, Fitzgibbon Nursery."
   "Do you offer lawn-care service?"
   "No, not for existing lawns,
but we do offer ongoing care of things we sell."
After replacing his old in-ground sprinklers,
removing the mature shrubs,
and planting new trees, flowers, and replacement bushes,
Dean was considered eligible for total yard care.
A crew of three men came two hours once a week.

When Dean opened the first statement,
   he learned what *buyer beware* meant:
$37 per person per hour,
times two hours a week,
times three people,
times four visits,
equaled $888 for the month.
The first visit of the new month had already occurred,
the second was that day.

"Hello, Fitzgibbon Nursery."
   "I want to cancel my lawn service at the end of today."

An elderly neighbor across the street watched from behind her curtains
   as a man going door to door
was rebuffed at every other house on the block,
until he came to Dean's and Lana's.
Foster wanted short-term work.
He presented himself in a white, collared shirt and khakis
As a smooth, quick talker who nodded his head *yes* a lot.
The bushes, the flowers, the hedges, the lawn were "No problem."
He could do it in two hours, two days a week.
He was there next morning when Dean and Lana left.

Before nine o'clock he was gone.
His ploy had been to plump a few bulky trimmings
into numerous small lawn bags
and stack them at the curb.

Second morning he came again as Dean and Lana left.
Less than thirty minutes later,
Dean had been detained at the mall because
of an order not yet ready at the copy center.
While drinking a cup of coffee in the food court,
behind his back,
a man with a familiar voice approached a couple at the next table
and began pitching an Herbalife franchise.
It was Foster.
He was a huckster in a pyramid scheme.
Dean walked to the table,
plunked down a twenty-dollar bill and said,
"This is what my lesson cost me,
I advise you to leave before yours costs more."

Delano was up-front about having two jobs.
He turned meters on and off for the city water department
eight to five Mondays through Fridays.
On his way home from work and on Saturdays,
he edged and blew away the trimmings in yards
his wife, son, and daughter
had mowed earlier in the day.

Elsewhere,
Thirty years after retiring from teaching to keep house,
Lisa returned from the grocery store one day and found a note:

> *I don't love you anymore; I haven't for a long time. The cat, a thousand dollars I left in the checking account, and the house are yours. Get a job and make a new life for yourself.*
> *Bill*

After long cries of sorrow and despair,

her blackness lifted enough
to begin a personal inventory:
1. Ineligible for unemployment compensation
2. An ailing mother
3. Childless and without siblings
4. One hobby—gardening

Hmm, gardening.
Realtors might be able to use someone with gardening experience
to spruce up properties before their open houses.

Dean made a quick U-turn back to the empty house
with a *For Sale* sign in the yard,
where he saw Lisa deadheading flowers.
He hired her on the spot to do the same for him.

Spring, summer, and soon it was Labor Day.
Once a week Delano cut the lawn,
and Lisa did everything else.

Before the first frost,
Lisa's mother,
in the increasing throes of dementia,
began calling Lisa
to immediately return home for real and imagined crises.
Delano's children were back in school,
his wife could not do the mowing by herself,
and it was getting too dark after work for him to help her.
He began taking long lunch hours out of touch with the dispatcher.
The city manager soon called him in and told him to stop moonlighting
or lose his job.

After thirteen years,
a prairie-style ranch house
on a beautiful one-acre corner lot in the second-nicest part of town
was again for sale.

When asked why,

Dean and Lana pleasantly smiled and said, "To move closer to our grandchildren."

The truth was . . .
the yard had become too damn much trouble!

Rusty

In midsize towns,
Before suburbs were called additions,
When neighborhoods were an assortment
Of small, dissimilar, working-class houses
With front yards bisected by a ribbon of cracked, pitted sidewalk
Between elm trees in the "parking"
And space before porches where people actually sat in the evenings,
Seven-year-old children
Walked to and from school by themselves
And went home for lunch.
I was such a kid.

The only thing I worried about
Was finding Padgett's glint-eyed chow
Crouched in the dry, powdered dirt.
He growled deep, muffled threats
And dared me to pass where I had to go.
Although it was a public sidewalk,
My first step on the boundary
Was his cue to bolt to the length of his chain,
Inches from my escaping heels.

Thereupon, Padgett would call through her screen door,
"Don't worry, he won't bite."
That was easy for her to say!

Smile at Life

If it is moving so slowly you can't see it happen,
Don't take your eyes off of it.
Sooner than later has an expiration date.
Either it is done now
Or it's not done at all.

Ode to a Forthcoming Doctoral Dissertation

"I waked up,
And there me are."
At two years, eleven months,
Disregarding vocabulary limitations,
The thought is logically precise.

He runs up and down the hall,
And one day will go to kindergarten.
Educators will begin the twenty-plus-year task
Of teaching him to express complexity as simply
As when here he was.

Upon Reflection

A line of green trash carts at the curb
Waited like soldiers at attention
To feed the clanking, earsplitting behemoth
Gobbling along several streets away.

Extra trash bundled in distended plastic bags
Had been put out at the last minute
To reduce the possibility that marauding dogs and crows
Would strew debris helter-skelter.

Objects too large to cart or bag
Were piled alongside,
Available for inspection and plucking
By flea market vendors scouting the neighborhood.

A jogger approaching from two blocks away
Saw a pickup stop beside the discards.
The driver hopped out for a closer look at something,
Then drove on empty-handed.

When the intrigued jogger came upon the scene,
His nonchalant gaze revealed
The scavenger had rejected a charcoal grill that looked like new.
Desire to have it got the best of him.

Hightailing it home,
He barged into the kitchen and exclaimed to his wife,
"I just saw a nice charcoal grill in the trash.
Come, help me get it!"

Concerned someone they knew might see them,
They pulled their car even with the green carts to obscure the heist,
Got out, opened the trunk,
And proceeded to take the grill.

As they hoisted it over the bumper,
The bottom of the rusted firebox gave way.

Years' accumulation of damp, caked ash and millions of ants
Spilled into the trunk, onto them, and over the street.

What to do?
Someone must be watching!
Should they tediously muscle the grill back out of the car and drop it on the street,
Or leave immediately?

The grill's legs kept the trunk from closing.
It banged up and down over the slightest bumps.
If that indignity were not enough,
Ants were crawling over their entire bodies like animated measles.

In their anguish, he began to laugh hard.
"I am remembering what my dad told me the first day he took me to Joyland Park:
'A sidelined rollercoaster reveals nothing about the actual experience
Of its bottom falling out.'"

1956

Dr. Ellis was an intimidating man with privileged authority.
The only child of a German immigrant
Who made millions wildcat drilling for oil on scrub prairies,
He was stocky and clean-shaven
With ruddy cheeks and piercing blue eyes.
He had a loud, deep voice and a sinister laugh
That turned on and off in an instant.
Thousands of skeet shots had filled his wood-paneled den
With state and regional trophies
And gave him a nearly deaf right ear he refused to accept.
He thought people mumbled and spoke *too damn softly*.
"Speak up" was his standard retort to strangers.

He successfully invested in the stock market,
Owned a strip mall,
Bought a hilly farm,
Dammed the creek,
And built many luxury homes around the gated, man-made lake.
The mayor and the governor would take his calls.
He did everything in a big way.
He had a workshop full of industrial-grade power tools he seldom used.
Large fish tanks behind portholes in his bedroom wall
Were tended three times a week by people he never saw.
A pool table in a room with a fireplace was dark most of the winter.
His latest acquisitions were a powerboat and water toys.

A lad from the other side of town met Dr. Ellis's son
In the socially equalizing environment of a high school government club.
They played some pick-up basketball,
Target practiced a couple of times with .22s,
And dragged Main Street
In a six-year-old pale yellow Oldsmobile 98 convertible
With red leather seats
Dr. Ellis had passed down to his son when he turned seventeen.
One day they drove it to Dye's Supermarket

For a six-bottle carton of Coca-Cola.
While there, one of them out of need and the other on a whim,
Asked for and got jobs as checkout clerks.

Working different schedules except on Saturdays,
Their socialization dwindled back into casual contact at school.
So when the surprise invitation came
To fill a vacancy in an upcoming Ellis family summer vacation at a lake resort,
The boy, who lived with his father in a four-plex apartment,
Anguished over the rare opportunity,
Until his dad encouraged him to accept.
Accustomed to evaporation by hot air turbulence through rolled-down windows,
He quickly found the air-conditioned two-tone yellow and white
Chevrolet Bel Air Nomad station wagon,
Pulling a 14-foot Lone Star runabout boat with a 50-horsepower Evinrude engine,
The epitome of luxury.

He had never been in a powerboat,
Skied neither snow nor water,
And was secretly afraid of aquatic depths.
Yet, bound and determined to succeed,
He sputtered and struggled to secure one foot,
And then the other, in the skis' bindings.
Bobbing in the water like an unstable cork
As the boat slowly circled around him,
He caught the rope from behind,
Thrust it over his head into the shaky V between his skis,
And let it slide through his curled fingers
Until he latched on to the wooden grip at the end.

It amazed him how fast the slack disappeared
And the idling engine dragged him along.
Wobbling side to side,
Determined with all his might not to capsize,
He willed to keep his knees bent, skis straight,

And the rope in the middle.
When he said, "Hit it!"
Dr. Ellis shoved the throttle forward
Delivering full power from the Evinrude.
It flopped him headfirst right out of his skis.
Again and again he tried.
Neither he nor Dr. Ellis would admit defeat.
. . . and then he was up.

Twice around the cove at less than half throttle,
He stayed directly behind the boat,
Rigidly gripping the rope handle,
Stiffly crouching forward,
Unable to stand upright,
He precariously teetered side to side like a toddler taking his first steps.
Sputtering in the wake,
Burning in his muscles,
He was attached to the boat like a kite tail
Until Dr. Ellis cut the power
And dropped him beside the dock.

Then it was the first Brantley girl's turn.
Her family had flown their V-tail Beechcraft Bonanza
To a landing strip near the lake,
Like they had several times before.
She effortlessly slipped her feet into a set of trick skis
And entered the water from a dock start
Like a jet-propelled swan.
She pulled far out of the wake,
Nearly beside the boat,
Gracefully took the four-foot-high floating jump,
Then, changing the rope from one hand to the other,
Spun backward and forward several times.

Next, her sister attacked the slalom course left and right.
Her high wakes,
Thrown like a barber stropping a straight razor,

Doused everyone on the dock when she flew past.
Dr. Ellis's son got the rope next and skied well,
But not as well as the girls.
The boy with no ability was so embarrassed
That when his turn came again,
He deferred the opportunity until another day,
And said to Dr. Ellis,
"I'm a little sore.
Let them go and I'll ride shotgun."

With a windbreaker, bucket hat, zinc oxide, and sunglasses for protection,
He quickly mastered the skiers' hand signals
And relayed them into Dr. Ellis's good ear.
360 degrees around,
But mainly to the sides and to the stern,
He spotted and pointed out swimmers, other skiers, and other watercraft.
Dr. Ellis was glad to have the help
And found his job was easier
As the boat buffeted along,
When he was able to give undivided attention
To the choppy water ahead
Rather than constantly checking a skier behind him.

After the last run and the boat was secured,
Everybody was tired and sweaty.
The girls stayed on the dock and sunbathed,
The boys went to their room and took a nap.
About sundown,
After everyone had a chance to shower and get ready,
They went into town for dinner,
Strolled through some shops,
And were back home in bed by ten.

When the vacation has been recalled in the years since,
That evening was unremarkable.
What they all remember is breakfast the next morning.

The two families shared a three-story duplex in the pocket of a cove.
The second floor opened between the units
Into a large dining room.
By six thirty everyone was up,
Rising sun streamed through panoramic windows along the deck,
The sideboard abounded with breakfast fare,
And the table was set with a cloth and fancy napkins.
The only seat left was directly across from Mr. Brantley,
Next to Dr. Ellis, who sat at the head of the table.
The boy took the empty chair and remained silent, eating his oatmeal and toast.
Abruptly, Dr. Ellis turned to him and said,
"Today you will cross the wake."
"I will try."
"What? Speak up, lad."
"I will try."
"You will DO it!"
"Yes, I will do it."

On the boy's other side,
One of the Brantley girls was peppering her scrambled eggs with little success.
In the high humidity, holes in the shaker were partially plugged.
Nothing but fine dust was puffing out.
An overhead fan gently wafted some of the dust into the boy's nostrils
Just as he lifted a spoonful of oatmeal to his lips.
KERCHOO!
Oatmeal spat across Dr. Ellis's plate
Onto Mr. Brantley's shirt,
Contaminating bacon and eggs and the tablecloth as it went.
The room fell silent.
Nothing moved except the overhead fan
And Dr. Ellis's head as he looked down at his meal.
Mr. Brantley started to swear.
The boy remained transfixed.

Then, from somewhere deep within himself,
Dr. Ellis started a laugh

That became a guffaw,
That grew into paroxysmal coughing.
When he eventually caught his breath,
Between intermittent chuckles,
Which were now joined by everyone except Mr. Brantley,
Dr. Ellis said,
"I always wanted to do something like that,
But I never did.
You're all right, boy,
You're all right!"

A Typical Day

The summer after World War II ended
Troops were coming home,
Prosperity was about to begin again.
To be six years old was the greatest thing in the world.

The second-floor apartment
Had reached ninety degrees by noon,
And the temperature was rising faster inside than outside
Because the kitchen oven was on.

Eric's mother, in a housedress and bib apron,
Added four eggs
And counted a hundred strokes to herself
As she beat the chocolate scratch-cake batter smooth.

An Emerson fan swept hot air
Back and forth across the room,
But the heat was of no concern to Eric,
Who eagerly waited to lick the bowl and wooden spoon.

Awhile later he and two friends
Sat under the shade of sumac trees behind the house next door,
Trying to decide what to do with themselves
Until it was time for his birthday party.

His dad told him yesterday was so hot
The radio station announcer said
You could fry an egg on the sidewalk.
Today was just as hot.

The more they thought about it,
The more they concocted a game,
Not of eggs, but of mud.
Who could cook the fastest mud pie?

Tommy got a bucket and shovel,
Connie got three empty coffee cans,

Eric got an empty longneck milk bottle full of water,
And they were off to find the perfect dirt.

It took fine, black granules
And a specific ratio of water
To make the creamy, cement-like mix
They plopped in cookies on the retaining wall.

After cleaning their utensils with a hose,
And spraying themselves in the process,
They returned to the hot wall.
The pies were not yet dry.

So they climbed the mulberry tree.
More than halfway up
They sat on the shady branches
And ate as many ripe berries as they could reach.

Climbing back down,
They discovered a dead bird.
No one had told them they should not touch such a thing,
So they decided to bury it.

Tommy emptied an old cigar box of stuff,
Connie picked flowers through a neighbor's fence,
Eric got toilet paper in which to wrap the carcass,
And they dug a hole beneath the tree.

"God bless this bird and its family. Amen."
They covered up the box with dirt,
Placed the flowers on top,
And made a tombstone cross of two sticks.

After Mrs. Mayhew called Tommy home,
Eric and Connie talked a little longer
—about Connie's grandmother's expensive new false teeth—
Then they went home.

Their dads returned from work,
The three families ate their suppers.

Eric's mother wrapped a lucky dime in wax paper
And hid it in the cake.

It was time for his party.
Tommy and Connie and their parents came.
They brought presents, ate cake,
And Mr. Miller got the lucky dime.

That night the mud pies lay dry and cracked on the retaining wall,
The bird in the box was dug up by a cat,
And Mr. Miller had good luck;
He rescued his mother-in-law's new upper denture from the family dog.

Birds of a Feather

On a beautiful October Monday
At Ristorante Italiano
Inside seating was half-full at 12:15,
But the outside umbrella tables were empty.
Two young, hotshot attorneys hastened from courthouse recess,
Each in a black trim-cut suit, white shirt, and foulard tie,
Each a folder in hand,
Impatiently waited for the host to seat them.

"Outside, please."

"Water, or something else to drink?"

"Water."

"The same."

A minute or two later a waiter came
With bread, olive oil, and balsamic vinegar.
"I will give you a chance to look at the menu
And I'll be back."

"Okay."

Opening their folders,
Peeling out their yellow legal pads,
Neil said,
"I think we're airtight on 1 and 2.
The second point on 3 is still conjectural.
Even more damning is that zinger Todd threw us.
We've got to discredit and bury him with his own facts."

"Pardon me,
Have you decided?"

"Yes.
A ten-inch pepperoni pizza,

Two salads with house dressing,
And two glasses of your house Chianti."

Neil and Jeff thought, connived, wrote,
Revised, and rewrote their strategy.
Almost unnoticed,
The waiter brought the wine and salads,
And a few minutes later, the pizza.

"Have we missed anything?"

"No, I don't think so."

"Good."

"Okay, let's send it to Eleanor to clean up, print,
And deliver to the courtroom at one thirty."

Jeff took out his cell phone,
Touched the camera icon
And was framing the first page
When a bird swept out of nowhere
Into the basket of bread.
Lurching back,
The cell phone squirted from his grip
Into his untouched glass of water.
Simultaneously, Neil flipped his napkin at the basket
With more gusto than he intended.
Jeff's wine glass toppled onto the legal pads
And splashed Chianti down the front of his white shirt.
Both men jumped up from the table.

"Waiter! Waiter!"

In the ensuing chaos,
None of the three could decide what to do first.
Jeff was incredulous.
All he could think was,
Get my phone out of the water!

Look at me!
How am I going to go back to court?

All Neil could think was,
What the hell?
The notes are ruined!

The waiter,
Trying to mop Jeff with a napkin,
Was strongly shoved away with an elbow.

More waitstaff raced out from inside.
With napkins they grabbed somewhere along the way,
They attempted to sop up the table,
As Neil violently shook the two purple legal pads
All over them, himself, and everything else around.

Meanwhile, the bird, joining many of its kind
Perched in a tree shading the parking lot,
Waited for a chance at another morsel,
And bombarded black-and-white splats onto the seats
Of Neil's brand new red Corvette convertible.

Charity Begins at Home

At the end of World War II, home-front support workers and their families
Still lived on the block of two-story residences
Converted into four or more apartments each.

As financial recovery was underway,
More food on the tables and refrigerators to replace iceboxes
Consumed a large portion of increasing disposable incomes.

Brian was seven.
His father, mother, and he lived on the second floor.
The stairs were straight without a door at the top.

Tinker was six.
His family lived around the corner in a basement apartment.
He had three younger siblings and another on the way.

When Brian outgrew his leather oxfords,
There was still good wear in them.
The toes and lateral sides of Tinker's shoes had nearly rubbed away.

Brian and his mother gave the oxfords a double polishing,
And washed and stretched the cotton laces.
They were excited for the surprise.

When Tinker next came to play,
He went home for supper wearing Brian's outgrown oxfords,
His own worn-out shoes in hand.

Tinker was happy.
Brian was happy.
Brian's mother was happiest of all.

Less than ten minutes later
There was a knock at the door and Brian raced down the stairs to answer.
He looked through the glass.

"Mom, it's Tinker!"

"Let him in."
And he did.

Angry as a dog whose bone had just been taken away,
He threw Brian's oxfords, one after the other, as hard as he could, up the stairs, saying,
"WE DON'T WANT YOUR DAMN SHOES!"

Instant Rebate

"Honey,
I'm going to Pencils to buy some tape and pens,
Do you need anything?"
"No, we are all right."
"Before I go,
I think I will check online to see if they have any coupons.

They do.
They have an instant fifty percent rebate on a box of copy paper.
Five thousand sheets are a bit excessive,
But this is a terrific deal.
I'll print the coupon and get us a box."

Three passing clerks asked the same thing:
"Do you need help finding anything?"
"No, I have a short list, I am doing fine."
I found the stack of paper under a sign that read:
Buy One Box and Get the Second One at Half Price.

Since the online offer said
Fifty Percent Off One Box, Limit Two,
It was logical that a coupon in hand for one box at half price
Superseded a deal for twenty-five percent off two boxes.
Furthermore, I only wanted one box.

I loaded a box of paper into my cart.
Somewhere along my way in life,
I once knew, but had apparently forgotten,
A deal that seems too good to be true
Might well be.

At the checkout stand,
The clerk said, "Did you find everything?"
"Yes, I came for the tape and pens,
But couldn't turn down the paper deal.
Here is my coupon."

Ka-ching, ka-ching, ka-ching.
"How does the instant rebate on the paper work?"
Churning out a receipt over two feet long, he said,
"I don't know, take this over there to her, and she will help you,"
And he abruptly turned around and left.

In the adjacent checkout stand,
After she finished with her customer,
I was next.
She greeted me with a smile.
Her badge said *STORE MANAGER*.

"The fellow who just left the cash register over there
Said to see you about my instant rebate on this paper."
"May I see your receipt?"
"Yes."
"It doesn't say anything about a rebate."

"He kept the coupon.
I got the box of paper at your big display against the back wall.
The sign on the stack said *Buy One Box and Get the Second One at Half Price,*
But my coupon said
Fifty Percent Off, Limit Two, Instant Rebate."

The clerk who checked me out was skirting around the end of an aisle.
"That's the fellow who took my coupon."
She said, "I will have someone else in the back check the stack."
Picking up a phone, she paged throughout the store,
"Earl, check the price on the paper display for SKU 513096."

The three-foot banner he brought forward read:
Buy One Box and Get the Second One at Half Price.
"I know, but my coupon said I could purchase one box
And receive an instant rebate for fifty percent."
The manager said, "Let's cancel the order and start over."

"Earl, take him back to the online kiosk,
See if you can find the offer he is talking about."

Together Earl and I did find it.
The computer stated it was an *online* offer
That included free shipping to my home.

This was the deal I wanted.
I slid my credit card through the reader.
The printer churned out another two-foot-long receipt.
Then I said to Earl,
"How do I get my rebate?"

He unfurled the receipt
And looked through the fine print—top to bottom.
There was not one word about a rebate.
"When you get home,
Call the hotline number here at the bottom."

"No, let's do it now on my speakerphone."
I handed it to him and he dialed the number.
While his computer screen was holding the transaction details,
Suddenly a decrementing popup flashed over them:
Screen will close in 10 . . . 9 . . . 8 . . . seconds.

Phone in one hand while he responded to a chain of automated choices,
He wavered to touch the popup reset icon with three seconds remaining.
At about the same moment an all-too-familiar recording on the phone said,
We are experiencing an unusually large number of calls at this time,
Please hold for the next available operator.

Over and over during the monotonous melody that followed,
The decrementing popup returned:
Screen will close in 10 . . . 9 . . . 8 . . . seconds.
Earl kept it alive until his attention wandered off somewhere,
And I caught the dead-man icon just before it reached zero.

Twelve more minutes lapsed on the phone's clock.
Earl burst out,
"Hello? Hello? Somebody answer!"
Of course, nobody did.
He continued to reset the computer screen.

Finally, the music stopped.
It roused both of us from a stupor.
"Thank you for waiting.
This is Loobleoop"—an unintelligible name pronounced at lightning speed—
"How may I help you?"

Earl explained the whole thing.
Loobleoop said he had to put us on hold to find an answer.
The monotonous loop of agglutinated melody resumed.
Three minutes later on the phone clock,
Loobleoop returned.

"What is the transaction number again?"
All sixteen digits verified, he said, "Got it!
The corresponding rebate number is 13-QB561.
Tell your customer to follow the online instructions at *Pencilsrebate.com*.
I hope this is helpful, have a good day." Click.

I told Earl thank-you and turned to leave.
He said, "Were you satisfied?"
I said, "I appreciate you sticking with me."
He quickly drew a card from a plastic caddy beside the computer
And wrote his own *excellent* service report.

Smiling to myself on the way back to the front of the store,
I saw the manager talking with two of her employees.
She called out to me, "Did you get everything taken care of?"
"It apparently will be after I get to my computer.
Earl couldn't finish the job back there."

"I can do it for you here at the counter."
She entered my personal information,
The SKU number, the order number, and the rebate number.
"Would you like a copy of the rebate confirmation?"
"Yes, I would."

"The box of paper will arrive at your home within two days.
Save your receipt and the copy of the rebate confirmation.

If you don't receive your rebate in the mail,
Bring these back
And we will get it taken care of."

"Thank you.
If I haven't gotten the rebate in a couple of weeks,
I will be back."
"Oh, no. It will take much longer than that.
Look at the rebate confirmation form I just gave you."

This is what it said:
Your rebate request has been submitted for final validation,
But payment has not yet been approved.
This process takes approximately 8-10 weeks.
Thank you for shopping at Pencils.

Bee

On the patio table
It seeks food from the plate
I choose not to share.
Despite fanning and shooing,
It will not go away.
It has the entire yard of flowers on which to feast;
Why does it persist in being a nuisance?

Although I risk the wrath of its stinger,
My patience is running out.
This is the moment that precedes the moment
When enough is enough.
For both our sakes,
I wish it sensed now is the time to forget the present
And think about the future.

Campaign Trail

Enter any time, any day,
—it makes no difference in which direction—
A dog lying in wait
Inside a yard on the eastern slope of the canyon
Barks multiple times,
And no quicker than done,
While he gathers breath for another barrage,
His echo lingers a fraction of a second from the other side.

Thinking it is another dog,
He barks louder and quicker
In a cacophonous spiral of ignorance.
For a hiker walking onward,
With increasing distance behind,
The way ahead becomes deceptively quiet
Until, crossing a culvert to the western rim
Another dog in another yard launches into an identical barking fit.

Progressing to the widest divergence of the chasm,
More dogs on both sides quickly join the fray,
Until the whole neighborhood is involved:
Left, right, and center.
Not one of them realizes that half of the barking is an echo,
Or that each contributor
Is so busy making his own statement,
He fails to notice the reason to bark has already passed by.

Get Up

Awakened at 6:45 by loud squawking
And vigorous whacking,
I quickly turned in bed toward the high open window.
The tops of three pines against the bluing sky were empty.
The action was lower down.

Getting up to peer over the sill,
I saw two hikers had returned from the woods.
Dad was standing by to watch
As his one-year-old son yelled and pounded with open palms
On the side of his grandpa's cabin.

Four Crayons, Ten Minutes

Children draw crescent moons and full moons
With smiling faces above things like blue houses and green dogs,
And then they fidget.

Mothers draw suns and curlicue clouds
With smiling faces above things like green firemen and red turtles,
And hope the mac and cheese comes soon.

Departure

Arose before dawn.
Dew on everything under a clear sky.
Bed made.
African violet watered.
Light on bedside table off.
New pebble left on windowsill.
Return station dial on radio to where it was.
No footprints on carpet.
Wadded bags from shopping put in kitchen trash.
Thank-you card on kitchen table.
Visual scan to remember another year, another year.
Three of the family stand on the porch to say good-bye.
Luggage in rental car trunk.
Tap horn at the road.

About the Author

Richard J. Ackerman Jr. was born and reared in Middle America, where he attended public schools and university. He served three years as a dentist in the U.S. Air Force during the Vietnam War, and later, after completing specialty training and a postdoctoral research fellowship at Harvard University, he was an orthodontic educator for twenty-one years. Upon retirement, the rank of professor emeritus was bestowed upon him by the University of Missouri Kansas City. The following thirteen years he practiced orthodontics full-time in southwest Kansas. Then he set aside dentistry and began to write. This is his first book. Dr. Ackerman and his wife divide their time between Carlsbad, California, and Estes Park, Colorado. They have two grown children and three grandchildren.

www.ingramcontent.com/pod-product-compliance
Ingram Content Group UK Ltd.
Pitfield, Milton Keynes, MK11 3LW, UK
UKHW041952230426
12048UKWH00008B/302